DATE DUE

DE 2 0 '00			
JL 22 02			
AP 6 '04			

DEMCO 38-296

THE PICASSO PAPERS

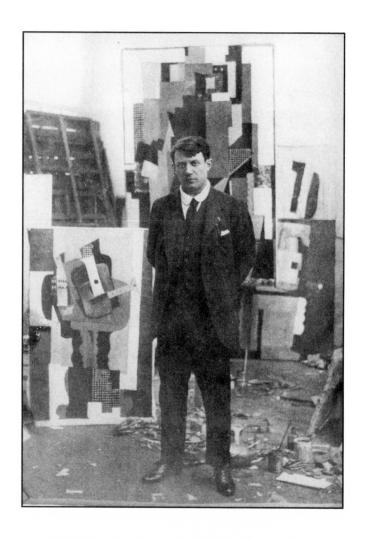

Self-Portrait in front of *Man Leaning on a Table*
and *Guitar, Clarinette, and Bottle on a Guéridon,*
in the rue Schoelcher Studio, Paris,
1915–16

THE

PICASSO

PAPERS

ROSALIND E. KRAUSS

Farrar, Straus and Giroux

New York

Farrar, Straus and Giroux
19 Union Square West, New York 10003

Library of Congress Cataloging-in-Publication Data
Krauss, Rosalind E.
    The Picasso papers / Rosalind E. Krauss.—1st ed.
        p.   cm.
    ISBN 0-374-23209-1 (cloth : alk. paper)
    1. Picasso, Pablo, 1881-1973—Criticism and interpretation.
    2. Collage, French.   3. Cubism—France.   I. Title.
    N6853.P5K73   1998
    759.4—dc21   97-16471

For Denis

CONTENTS

ILLUSTRATIONS

INTRODUCTION

A PENNY FOR

PICASSO

Mr. Olier-Larouse's car has killed old Mr. Montgillard, as he was out walking in Charolles.

—Fénéon, "News in Three Lines"[1]

W E SMILED WRYLY AT WARHOL'S REMARK about everybody, in the future, being famous for fifteen minutes. We accepted it as a comment on our modernity, which is to say our postmodernity, since the little statement, uttered almost at the end of the twentieth century, seemed to address a universal lust for notoriety born with and nurtured by television.

And yet, at the very beginning of the century, it was the culture of print journalism, in the form of the massively expanding circulation of daily newspapers, that fed the same fantasies. A little surge of fame buoyed the protagonist of the *fait-divers*, or local news item, making him or her more than just the victim of an accident, or the perpetrator of a crime, or the hero of a rescue. Producing a compensation for the unlucky or a reward for the brave in the form of a "story," the news item propelled its subject out of anonymity to become, no matter how briefly, a public character.

Perhaps it was this very brevity and the irony of its inverse relation to the mass circulation through which the little story would flit by its readers that led Félix Fénéon in 1906 to spin for *Le Matin*, the paper for which he worked, his own version of the *fait-divers*, his "news in three lines." Thus: "Love. In Mirecourt, a weaver, Colas, planted a bullet in the head of Mlle. Fleckenger, then treated himself with equal severity."[2] Or: "Silot, a valet in Neuilly, installs a lady of pleasure during his master's absence, then disappears, taking everything—except her."[3]

There is another irony besides the speed with which Fénéon is working, of course. It has to do with what Jean Paulhan calls, in his introduction to Fénéon's *Collected Works*, this haiku-like, punctual form of "unity" which, in its purported classicism, confers a "point" on these narratives that they would not otherwise have. "For by their very nature the *faits-divers* are absurd," Paulhan writes. "We learn of the existence of Mr. Dupont on the day when this man falls from a moving train or lets himself be killed by his wife. There you have the least interesting event that took place in Mr. Dupont's life. (For one dies of a little mishap, but it is truly hard to live.)" Thus in Fénéon's hands the *fait-divers* is a fake narrative, which, if it inspires novels, must do so fraudulently and in the form of a betrayal since, Paulhan points out, "if nature always ends, as they say, by resembling art, we need to stress that it resembles it badly."[4]

It was at around the same moment when Fénéon was gently mocking the *fait-divers* that André Gide cut three such stories from various papers—the first two from the *Figaro* and the *Journal de Rouen* in September 1906, both telling of a coin counterfeiting ring whose members included the young sons of ranking bourgeois families, the third from the *Journal de Rouen* of June 5, 1909, recounting a schoolboy's suicide after he and his companions drew lots. Carrying these stories around in his wallet until the late teens, when he began to sketch the ideas for what would become his novel *The Counterfeiters*, Gide admonished himself to "weld this [material] into a single homogeneous plot."[5]

In the first of the notebooks tracking the book's conception, Gide imagines using some of the reported testimony from the counterfeiters' trial as the motto for the opening of his novel—the response by one Fréchaut, when asked if he was a member of the "gang": "Let's call it 'the coterie,' your honor," he replied warmly. "It was a gathering where we dealt in counterfeit money, I don't deny that; but we were principally concerned with questions of politics and literature" (410).

This relation of counterfeiting to literature, in which the problem of certain forms of writing is metaphorized not through the pointlessness of the *fait-divers* but through the worthlessness of the fake coin, is subsequently announced by Gide's hero, Edouard, as the initial idea for the book—"In reality, Edouard had in the first place been thinking of certain of his fellow novelists when he began to think of *The Coun-*

terfeiters" (191)—and since the novel Edouard is depicted as working on bears the same title as the one Gide is writing, the metaphor serves Gide as well as it does his hero.

But if the problem of the literary counterfeit is what Gide is addressing as he writes at the outset of the 1920s, he knows that in relation to the political economy—Fréchaut, after all, spoke of literature *and* politics—the fake gold coin can only play a role in a story set before the war, "since at present," he reminds himself, "gold pieces are outlawed" (413). This "present" is the immediate postwar period, in which one could still think that the wartime suspension of the circulation of gold money in France and England was temporary; in fact, however, the suppression of the gold standard was to be permanent and the inconvertibility of paper money was to become structural throughout modern societies.

The temporal knot in the metaphorical structure of *The Counterfeiters* is, then, that the fraudulence that interests its author, while symbolized by a fake gold piece, is in fact the result of a monetary system in which gold now plays no part, and what circulates instead are abstract tokens redeemable by no concrete value at all. If we think of aesthetic modernism itself as severing the connection between a representation (whether in words or images) and its referent in reality, so that signs now circulate through an abstract field of relationships, we can see that there is a strange chronological convergence between the rise of the inconvertible token money of the postwar economy and the birth of the nonreferential aesthetic sign.

This is the argument elaborated by Jean-Joseph Goux, in a series of books that explore Fréchaut's convergence between "politics and literature" by asserting a continuing structural homology between the two fields.[6] On the one hand, in the prewar period a literature of naturalism that assumed a transparency between language and its real-world referent runs parallel to a currency backed by (and thus also "transparent to") the real value of the gold coin; on the other hand, by the end of the teens a modernist literature that stakes its aesthetic integrity on the free play of its signifying elements is contemporary with an economic system entirely regulated by the abstract legal apparatus of banking through which token money circulates.

Now, if Gide falls into the anachronism of using the fake gold coin to symbolize the modernist system, it is because the object itself has a paradoxical value. For the thin sheathing of gold wash barely conceals its underlying crystal disk: "It has the brightness and the sound of a real piece," the character who presents it to Edouard says, "it is coated with gold, so that, all the same, it is worth a little more than two sous; but it's made of glass. It'll wear transparent. No; don't rub it; you'll spoil it. One can almost see through it, as it is" (192). Thus the object's worthlessness as money is the very thing that secures its value as aesthetic symbol, for it is the transparent crystal lying beneath the gilt that reaches toward the abstract, nonreferential, self-sustaining purity of the modernist work of art. And as Edouard says of the abstract novel he dreams of writing: "Purity is the only thing I care about" (74).

Rehearsing the reductionist logic so characteristic of modernism, in which an artist's duty is to find the essence of the medium in which he is working, which means leaving the inessential to other mediums—with painting, for example, ceding realistic representation to photography—Edouard reasons in the case of the novel that both dialogue and outward events can now be seen to belong to the cinema. "Even the description of the characters does not seem to me properly to belong to the *genre*," he argues (74). And in telling his friends about his ambition for this abstract novel of ideas, he adds, "What I should like to do is something like the art of fugue writing" (190).

This, however, is where Gide permits the fraudulent character of the coin proffered to Edouard to wash back over the crystalline condition of its purported "purity," as he compares the abstractions with which his novelist hero wants to fill his pages to the tokens of the money economy: "Ideas of exchange, of depreciation, of inflation, etc., gradually invaded his book (like the theory of clothes in Carlyle's *Sartor Resartus*) and usurped the place of the characters" (192). Which is to say that to the extent that *The Counterfeiters* is a novel of ideas, it is a fake novel, with—as one rubs off the gold of its seeming representation of persons and events—nothing at its center but glass. This is what Edouard's interlocutors warn him of, and it is something he also worries about, joined as he is by

Gide, who uses his characters to advance his own views on the subject.

For at the level of literature, fraudulence not only carries the threat that one might aim for purity yet end up making a fake *novel* but also heralds the danger that abstraction, trafficking in the token as an utterly empty sign, might lead to language that means nothing at all. This is the depth of fraudulence suggested by one of the book's villains, the counterfeiter Strouvilhou, who is also to become the editor of an avant-garde literary review. Proceeding to tie the knot between metaphorical counterfeiting and the monetary image—"If I edit a review, it will be in order to prick bladders—in order to demonetize fine feelings, and those promissory notes which go by the name of *words*" (332)—Strouvilhou also loops these strands through the postwar phenomenon of dada; the first issue, he announces, is to have "a reproduction of the *Mona Lisa*, with a pair of moustaches stuck on to her face" (372). It is this linking of abstraction and non-sense that is associated, in Gide's narrative, with the emptying out of the sign's meaning: "If we manage our affairs well," says Strouvilhou, "I don't ask for more than two years before a future poet will think himself dishonoured if anyone can understand a word of what he says. All sense, all meaning will be considered anti-poetical. Illogicality shall be our guiding star" (332).

Indeed, it was the very word *dada* that Gide understood as having achieved Strouvilhou's ambition. Gide's own magazine, the well established *N.R.F.*, which had recommended publication in 1919 after a five-year wartime hiatus, had immediately attacked the movement in an anonymous note accusing the "new school" of nonsense symptomatized by the "indefinite repetition of the mystical syllables 'Dada dadada dada da.' " Gide would personally join this attack the following year with an article announcing: "The day the word Dada was found, there was nothing left to do. Everything written subsequently seemed to me a bit beside the point. . . . Nothing was up to it: DADA. These two syllables had accomplished that 'sonorous inanity,' an absolute of meaninglessness" (*N.R.F.*, April 1920).[7]

Nonetheless Gide, who, as he liked to declare, had always "taken the most youthful movements and tendencies very seriously,"[8] was eager to court the goodwill of Breton, Aragon, and Soupault, and to publish material in their journal, *Littérature*, a review soon to proclaim its own allegiances to dada. In this sense Gide himself assumed the posture of his novel's primary example of the literary fraud, the wealthy Robert de Passavant, who, although a conventional novelist, wants to underwrite an avant-garde journal in order to ally himself with the latest trend. Aragon, indeed, became suspicious of Gide's apparent friendship early on ("Gide always has his finger in the wind"), as did others of the younger generation: "Gide takes an interest in everything, not just to amuse himself, but in a state of Baudelairean anxiety before the idol: Take care, it might be the real God."[9]

At its most pernicious level, the fraudulent is thus a corollary of the "empty sign," the outgrowth of what structural linguistics would call a "token" language, signs circulating without a "convertible" base in the world of nature. The result is not just a promiscuity of meanings that have become polysemic or sonorously empty but also the difficulty of determining genuine aesthetic value at all, the problem most "truly" endemic—according to some—to modernism.*

Both inside Gide's novel and in real life, then, the image of the counterfeit functions as a complex figure, a kind of pretzel in which true and false chase each other's tails. Glass and gold, pure and impure, begin to reflect on one another, as in a hall of mirrors. The nightmare projected by *The Counterfeiters* is that in this era of abstract token money, with no way for representation to touch base in gold, there is increasingly little way of telling the difference.

• • •

It was in 1919, the year Gide began to sketch his novel, that Picasso mounted a massive one-man show in Paris at the Paul Rosenberg Gallery, his first since 1905. Insofar as the exhibition, divided between cubist work and neoclassical drawing, drew down on itself charges of fraudulence, it represents a

---

*Addressing the increasingly hermetic discussions of modern music, Stanley Cavell writes, for instance: "What they suggest is that the possibility of fraudulence, and the experience of fraudulence, is endemic in the experience of contemporary music." And replying to those who say that genuine works of art will be separated out from false ones over the course of time, he adds: "But in waiting for time to tell that, we miss what the present tells—that the dangers of fraudulence, and of trust, are essential to the experience of art" (*Must We Mean What We Say?* [New York: Scribner's, 1969], 188).

watershed in Picasso's career. For in the eyes of those supporters like Wilhelm Uhde for whom the value—beyond its weight in gold—of Picasso's work was its modernism, which is to say the invention of cubism's spatially free-floating, almost nonrepresentational sign, the flirtation with classicism so apparent in the Rosenberg Gallery was a ghastly betrayal of those earlier aspirations.[10]

For Uhde, as for many art historians after him, the chronological knot that fascinated Gide, interweaving as it did postwar aesthetic dilemmas with prewar symbolic objects, could not have applied to Picasso's art, since it seemed perfectly apparent that the war years had simply split his work in two. The period up to 1914 represents a triumphant development of the cubist logic, which with the advent of collage increasingly fashions a visual sign free to circulate within pictorial space, independent of any fixed referent, and thus wholly inconvertible: a signifier-as-token, indeed, in free play. This is the modernist, "true" Picasso. But the postwar period, so significantly announced by the Rosenberg exhibition, is not only a return to the gold standard of visual naturalism. To the extent that this return via the imitation of a range of "classical" artists, from Poussin to Ingres to late Renoir, is conducted under the banner of pastiche, it has branded onto its very surface, as it were, the mark of its own fraudulence. Here is Picasso as counterfeiter, his act a blatant betrayal of the modernist project.

Perhaps the most far-reaching theoretical model of such a split between modernist purity and its counterfeit Other is the one Theodor Adorno constructed for the development of twentieth-century music by pitting Schoenberg's twelve-tone constructions against Stravinsky's system of pastiche.[11] For, as Adorno orchestrates this opposition, the issues are not just abstraction versus "naturalism" but what siding with the one or the other implies for the fate of the individual subject within technologized, and regimented, industrial culture.

The question of the subject is always in the foreground of Adorno's attention, but it is also what is raised by Stravinsky when he attacks Schoenberg's decision to secure the rights of subjectivity by means of the twelve-tone row. For if Schoenberg sees the row as the exercise of pure choice—freed from the limits of prescribed musical convention or conceptions of harmonic "naturalness" and freed, thus, into abstraction—Stravinsky condemns this exercise as mere arbitrariness. The twelve-tone row, Stravinsky would say, may indeed be set by the individual composer's will, but in being responsible to nothing, it exposes the very subject it is supposed to serve to his or her own emptiness (136).

Adorno's counterargument is that for the first time the row constitutes the technical material of music—pitches, tones, tempi, dynamics—as objective elements to be rationally constructed into a system and thus to be comprehended by the subject who has conceived it from inside the construction. Furthermore, he contends, the history of music itself is contained in this very occurrence in which the subject's self-understanding arises from a togetherness-in-opposition with the objectified material seemingly most alien to it.

If subjectivity in Western music came to be projected onto the sonata's development section, where "subjective reflection upon the theme . . . decides the fate of the theme" (55), this was because in freeing music from its dependence on conventions, development opened up a realm for the autonomous aesthetic subject. But a consequence of this move to organize music via sheer thematic development was the liberation of the dynamically independent voice from the homophonic chordal whole. As music progressed through the nineteenth century, dissonance extended this independence, becoming an ever more important resource for breaking into the unity of the chord in order to emancipate its separate elements and, by differentiating them, to give each a "voice."

Dissonance was thus not only a liberation from the grip of "nature's" consonance (harmony); as it produced an experience of the independent subject it also laid bare a sense of the objective nature of music as pure contrast, pure opposition: tempo against tempo, pitch against pitch. "Consequently," Adorno writes, "the subjective drive and the longing for self-proclamation without illusion becomes the technical organ of the objective work. On the other hand, the reverse is true as well; it is the rationality and the unification of the material which makes the subjected material tractable to the forces of subjectivity" (59).

The row, one could say, is dissonance made absolute, made nothing but contrast. Yet, in being so atomized, every single tone reflects the construction of the whole that determines it. If "dissonances arose as the expression of tension, contradiction, and pain," now within Schoenberg's music, "they take on fixed contours and become 'material.' They are no longer the media of subjective expression," Adorno writes. "For this reason, however, they by no means deny their origin. They become characters of objective protest" (86).*

Thus it is the inner logic of musical development that Adorno sees Schoenberg following. According to this logic, the very moves the subject makes to free him- or herself render the objective character of music's technical means ever more manifest and absolute. Adorno's answer to Stravinsky, then, is that nothing about this process or the music it entails is arbitrary.

But Stravinsky, he would say, reaps the consequences of the very same logic, though it is now contaminated by two refusals. The first is Stravinsky's denial that the polyphonic emancipation of the voice must ultimately lead to dissonance and finally to the end of tonality altogether; the second is his refusal to side with the subject against the mounting regimentation of the social field.

Retaining tonality, in no matter how "mutilated" a form, Stravinsky makes the history of the exhaustion of musical pos-

---

*About the principle of contrast Adorno writes, "The seismographic registration of traumatic shock becomes . . . the technical structural law of music. It forbids continuity and development. Musical language is polarized according to its extremes: towards gestures of shock resembling bodily convulsions on the one hand, and on the other towards a crystalline standstill of a human being whom anxiety causes to freeze in her tracks. It is this polarization upon which the total world of form of the mature Schoenberg—and of Webern as well—depends" (42).

sibility—and therefore the constriction of the individual—into the content of his work. If pastiche becomes his medium, with its constant parody at the melodic and rhythmic level—of fairground music, jingles, ragtime, tango, waltz—as well as at the level of the instrument—the hand organ, the toy horn—this is in response, Adorno says, to late-nineteenth-century composers' recourse to making music about music, as in Wagner's *Meistersinger* or Strauss's pastiches. Pastiche as an artistic practice thus expresses the subjective experience of the intolerable narrowing of the scope for invention due to the limitations inherent in an art's organizing structure, in this case the system of tonality and all that follows from it. Such limitations were made increasingly clear in the nineteenth century, as the rise of lieder disrupted the harmonic balance of the homophonic classical form; in coming to the foreground, the melodic voice exposed the closing out of possibility within the tonal system. "The scant material," Adorno writes of this moment at which invention becomes paramount, "was totally exhausted. [Composers] therefore absorbed the depletion of this supply into a subjective relationship and then constructed their thematic motives—more or less openly—as 'quotations' with the effect of the recurrence of the familiar. In Stravinsky," he adds, "this principle becomes absolute" (182).

It is thus the threatened individual—the failed soldier, the tribe's sacrificial victim—whom Stravinsky takes up as "subject," in a reflection of tonal music's own spent force. And it is against this subject that the borrowed music of the pastiche, imitating at one and the same time the most primitive social drives and, in the very mechanization of their sound, the most technologically inflected forces, will exert the destructiveness of its repeated blows, in the form of Stravinsky's rhythms.*

In Adorno's interpretive system, pastiche is, then, both the form and the content of Stravinsky's fraudulence—his fake modernism, which is nothing but a betrayal of real modernist procedures. For as the very *form* of externality, of reaching outside music's own developmental logic, pastiche mocks the modernist project of a self-realization achieved through control of what is internal to the medium itself. And this mockery is both a shrug of the shoulders, as though the internal logic were merely optional, and a false imitation, since "music about music" is the counterfeit version of modernist immanence. On the other hand, in its guise as the *content* of this same externality, pastiche asserts an almost endless access to "style" as a series of personal and capricious choices open to the artist-subject as a kind of consumer browsing among compositional options.

Adorno's version of the counterfeit coin would differ radically from Gide's. Insisting on the historical necessity of experiencing the crystal disk as true, he would regard the very aspiration toward the redeemable character of gold as false.

---

*The contrast Adorno sets up between the Expressionist Schoenberg of *Erwartung* (1909) and the Stravinsky of the *Sacre du Printemps* (1911) does not involve issues of the twelve-tone system, but rather of a temporality that either internalizes the experience of the bourgeois subject in all its (shocked) isolation, or attacks the subject in the form of rhythmic blows that moreover spatialize time itself.

The musical material—pitch, beat, timbre—free of all tonal "naturalism" and now circulating through the crystal's system of twelve-tone relationships, guided only by the abstract laws of contrast, takes on the tokenlike character of the monetary model or, in its linguistic dimension, the pure signifier as defined by Saussure. For when the meanings of words are no longer understood as positive terms, directly convertible to a natural object or referent, but are thought of as purely differential—in Saussure's words, as "relative, oppositive, and negative"—meaning itself becomes a function of the system rather than of the world.[12]

This is the same move toward "inconvertibility" that has been argued for the onset of cubist collage, with the sudden arbitrariness of each pictorial element—a piece of newsprint able alternatively to signify light or dust or wood or water, depending on its relationship to its neighboring elements—now generating an utterly structural idea of the work of visual art.[13] Picasso himself, from across the historical divide of his later career, looked back on collage with a kind of wonder. Kahnweiler records him in 1948, enthusing to Léger: "What idiots or cowards we must have been to have given that up! We had marvelous means at our disposal. . . . We used to have *that*, and then I went back to oils and you to marble."[14] Yet, as Uhde observed in 1919, it was not simply to oils that Picasso returned—though many would argue that his very attempt to translate collage into its enameled copy was a betrayal that came as early as 1913—but to the fraudulence of naturalism's gold wash. And this would in turn, according to

Adorno's logic, necessarily come to imply pastiched versions of a whole museumful of representational art.

The medium of Picasso's fraudulence is thus the same as Stravinsky's in that—as pastiche—it is an art about art that redoubles the idea of modernist immanence and self-reference but does so now in the register of content rather than at the level of form. Which is to say that with Picasso's neoclassicism, art becomes the *representational* content of art, whether by means of the sluggishly bloated nude imitating the look of archaic sculpture or the sleekly fashionable Olga restaging a portrait by Ingres. "Art" enters the work as an image rather than as what Adorno would call the "self-realization" of a historical process, which could only be registered structurally.

Adorno would undoubtedly have had something similar to say about Gide's *Counterfeiters*, in which the abstract novel is posited as the content of a book that clings to all the formal prerogatives of nineteenth-century naturalism: its psychologism, its spatial and temporal coherence, the objectivity of its narrator, even its attraction to the ballast of the "real" event, as represented by its kernel in the *fait-divers*. Like the fake gold piece that the story's protagonists pass from hand to hand, the novels pictured in a receding series of reflections within the novel—Edouard's author's within Edouard's, Edouard's within Edouard's narrator's, Edouard's narrator's within Gide's—produce the idea of circulatory free play as an *image*, always condemned to resist it as form.

• • •

Turning Gide's coin over and over in one's hand, examining now its crystal, now its gold, now its self-enclosure, now its external dependence, now its truth, now its fraudulence, one arrives at a way of thinking about Picasso. This is not just because Picasso, in deploying what can be seen as the earliest visual system of freely circulating signs, enters deeply into the crystal logic to be found in Gide's gold piece. Nor is such a parallel due solely to the way Picasso's later practice of pastiche falls victim—to an extent unmatched in the work of any other artist as great as he—to the condition of the counterfeit. Rather, it is the seeming interdependence of the two phenomena, as suggested by Adorno's model in which Stravinsky's recourse to parody is the dialectically necessary obverse of Schoenberg's interiorized process.

Something similar is posited when Jean-Joseph Goux argues that it is the very onset of token money that paradoxically carries fraudulence to the heart of the system. For if, as Gide himself notes, counterfeiting no longer makes sense at the level of the object once gold no longer circulates as money, counterfeiting nonetheless increases in intensity with the fall of the gold standard. Except that now it has risen to the level of the code, since it is the very law setting the value of the circulating paper that rules that this same law will offer no guarantee, no redeemability for this money. "The Law," Goux writes, "no longer guarantees any convertibility of signs even though they arise from its own site. . . . Thus the very site of Truth, the site of the transcendent code that ought to guarantee the relation between circulating signifiers and what they signify fully, and in reality, defaults."[15]

The "Penny for Picasso" is, then, double-edged. For it implies the inextricable historical linkage of the two sides of this coin. The task of what follows will be to explore the nature of this structure, examining each side individually and in terms of the necessity of their relationship, as the pure token gives way to fake gold. But the "penny" thus extended to Picasso cannot help being, as well, the sign of what Gide's hero feels invading his book: "ideas of exchange, of depreciation, of inflation, etc." Indeed, Picasso is the very model of the inflationary artist, not simply because prices for his work seem to be on a dizzying spiral ever upwards, but because as the great prestidigitator, the wizard who turns the debris around him—newspaper, withered leaves, bicycle parts—to creative account, he has been raised to the level of a Midas whose every touch is golden.

The price of this "inflation" has been to forget that the semiotic gold struck by turning newsprint into the sign for "light" or "air" is substantially different from the expensive mining of past art in service to the laws of pastiche, by which the linguistic coin of purity is reminted as the economic bonanza of the aesthetic fake. And so there is as well a welcome note of depreciation to be heard in this "Penny for Picasso," not unlike Eliot's faintly condescending "penny for the old guy." The splendor and misery, we could say, of the modern artist.

THE

CIRCULATION

OF THE SIGN

A T FIRST THEY SEEM TO ROTATE THROUGH THE crystalline atmosphere like so many weightless facets, the glinting light of an invisible gem. Now one of the fragments appears aqueous, like water beading the side of a bottle; now it dries to the shimmer of dust motes struck by a ray of sunlight . . .

. . . But then there arises the sound of voices. They speak of a political meeting, of market shares. Someone tells of a woman who poisoned her lover. "A chauffeur kills his wife," says another. Who says? Whose voice?

• • •

At first they seem to cycle through the crystal space like so many radiant facets of an absent jewel. Each newsprint fragment forms the sign for a visual meaning; then, as it butts against another, the sign re-forms and the meaning shifts.

From the buzz of tiny letters, black flecks on white, which in imitating the look of scumbled paint conjure the effect of air, to the crisply cut edge of an adjoining (or even of the same) sheet, which now hardens to the solid of a porcelain dish, each little paper piece submits itself to meaning, but never enduringly so. For the same piece, in another location, constellates another sign . . .

. . . But then, and from the very site of these signs, comes the sound of voices (Fig. 5). "Before long I saw the first corpse still grimacing with suffering; its face was nearly black," he says. "Then I saw two, four, ten, twenty; then I saw a hundred corpses." As he tells of the dead piled high on convoys and lying in ditches, he asks, "How many cholera victims did I come upon like this? Two thousand? Three thousand? . . . But I had seen nothing yet."[1] Who tells this story and in what tone? Is this tragedy or melodrama; is it empathy or exploitation? Is it war reporting or news blending imperceptibly into fait-divers? Is it joined to the battle reports the way the story about the soldier spitting out a bullet lodged in his head for twenty-six years abuts the news, a week or so later, of the peace ("Les Alliés signent l'Armistice. La Grèce s'abstient" December 4, 1912)?[2] Is it in the same tone as "In Fontaine-bleau, a tramp turns himself in for murder" (Fig. 10)—something straight out of Fénéon's "News in Three Lines"?

· · ·

At first they circulate through the crystalline space, its whiteness their "medium," both a real place and the abstraction of

a system. In one of the collages (Fig. 1), the circulatory movement is given physical form, since one of the fragments is the
other's twin—having originally been scissored from the same
sheet, so that, as in a jigsaw puzzle, both match along their
common edge—only now flipped relative to the other, back
to front. A pair, but nonidentical, unlike.

One of them, the lower, exploits the scrollwork of its left-
hand edge to assume the profile of a violin. Or rather half a
violin, since it depends on Picasso's drawn additions of bridge
and neck and right-hand side to elaborate the musical instrument. All by itself, however, notched as it is into the whiteness
of the sheet, a flattened shape set foursquare upon the page,
it declares itself allied with the support on which it lies: like
the sheet, it is physical, material, opaque; like the sheet, it is
resolutely frontal, facing its viewer. This is how the little fragment, in itself indeterminable, for it might be almost anything—bubbles of soda, stripes of shadow, rays of sun—
hardens and solidifies, its lines of writing now posturing as the
graining of wood. Thus the piece becomes the support, or
signifier, for a visual signified. Together they produce a meaning: the *density*, the *opacity* of a physical object, here, a violin.[3]

The circulation of the sign, however, is a rule of relativity.
And Picasso, here as elsewhere, abides by this rule. The second
newspaper fragment, placed above the violin's shoulders, deploys its own notches and curves to cup the pegs and scroll
of the instrument, becoming thus their "background." In this
position, the newsprint's lines of type now assume the look
of stippled flecks of graphite, the painter's visual shorthand for

atmospheric surround. A new place then summons forth a different sign. *Light* it declares, or *atmosphere*.

But the magic of the whole collage, indeed the brilliance of the game it plays, is that the two opposite meanings—*light* on the one hand and *opacity* on the other—are generated from the "identical" scrap of paper, the "same" physical shape. Like Saussure's phonetic substance, this support is seen to take on meaning only within the set of oppositions that pits one against another, the implosive *p* of *up* against the explosive *p* of *put*. Picasso's sheet, sliced in two, is thus a paradigm, a binary couple married in opposition, each taking on a meaning insofar as it is *not* the other. *Figure* and *ground* become this kind of contrary here, joined and redoubled by *opaque* and *transparent* or *solid* and *luminous*, so that just as one fragment is, literally speaking, the back side of the material from which the other was cut, the circulation of the sign produces this very same condition, but semiologically, at the level of the sign: *front, solid, shape; behind, transparent, surround.*

Does Picasso need to state any more clearly the sense in which the sign here, like the linguist's tokens, has no natural relation to a referent, no real-world model that gives it a meaning or secures its identity? Does he need to declare any more forcefully that here, in the fall of 1912, with his new medium of collage, he has entered a space in which the sign has slipped away from the fixity of what the semiologist would call an iconic condition—that of resemblance—to assume the ceaseless play of meaning open to the symbol, which is to say, language's unmotivated, conventional sign?[4] I like to think his

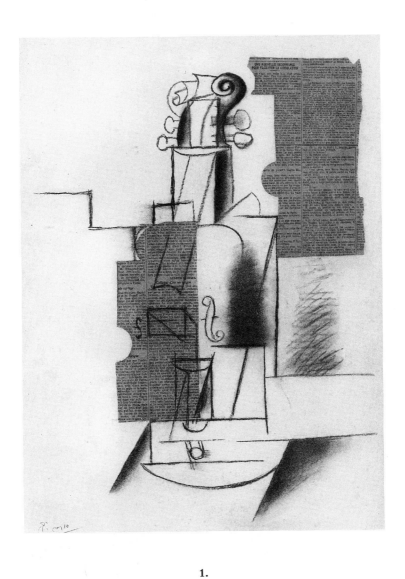

1.

Violin

autumn 1912

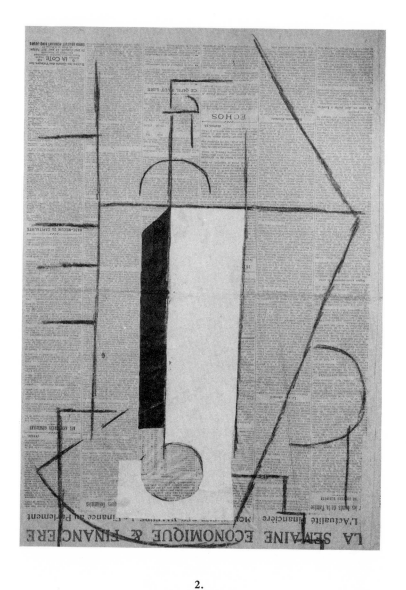

2.

Bottle on a Table

autumn–winter 1912

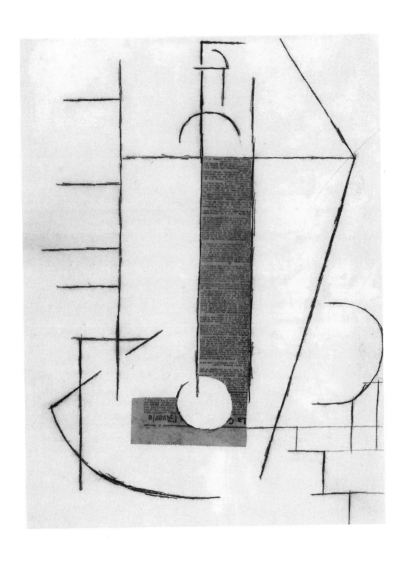

3.

Bottle on a Table

autumn–winter 1912

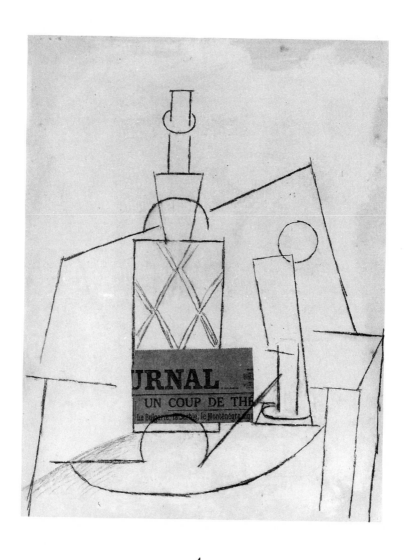

4.

Table with Bottle, Wineglass and Newspaper

autumn–winter 1912

answer to this comes in the form of the *f*-holes—the fortuitous lettering offered up to him by the real—since he writes with them, again and again, always placing one very large *f* in opposition to the other, very small. Penning them half on, half off the element that makes up the front face of the instrument, he inscribes them onto a surface that is resolutely flat, stolidly facing forward. It is their unequal size that then acts on this frontality, as it produces the sign for foreshortening, for the swiveling of the object into depth, like a door that is slowly swinging open. Scripting the *f*s onto the face of the violin, where manifestly there is nothing but flatness, Picasso writes *depth* onto an object set squarely before us and only as deep as a sheet of paper. "Depth," he says . . .

. . . But another depth speaks as well from the very surface of the newsprint fragment, the one onto which the *f*s are appended. This is the "depth"—historical, imaginative, political—of a place to which the word *Tchataldja* refers, the name of the battle site in the Balkans from which this dispatch was sent to *Le Journal*, Picasso's main source of newsprint—and, some would argue, of news.[5] It might have been *Podgoritza*, of course, or *Saint-Nicolas*, the datelines of accounts of the Balkan wars for articles that appeared at just this moment in the avant-garde magazine *Les Soirées de Paris*, signed by one of its editors, André Tudesq, a pal of Apollinaire's, and by Jérome Tharaud.

To listen to Tharaud is to picture the majestic isolation of the Montenegrin fighter, tall, gnarled, and armed to the teeth, perched on his mountain redoubt. This is the honor of the fighting clans, never submitted to the regimentation of the modern army but nonetheless ravaged, now, by Turkish guns.[6]

To listen to Tudesq is to hear strategy talked, a mapping of relations in space, to understand the way in which the battle for Saint-Jean de Medua is really a fight for Scutari, the prize the Montenegrins most covet and from which they will be excluded if the peace, about to be concluded, comes too soon. This is what King Nicolas fears: to be merely an onlooker when the Serbs and the Bulgarians share the spoils. The Montenegrin king began the adventure, writes Tudesq, as though he were watching an amusing film, with his son Prince Danilo gaily igniting the first canon. It's turned out badly. But not for the Serbs. Tudesq tells the story of a battle in which the Turks were routed. A pursuing Serb, obeying the rules of combat, asks a wounded soldier: "Christian or Muslim?" Receiving no answer he lops off the soldier's head. Of course, Tudesq adds wryly, he had "inconsiderately asked his question in Serbian: why didn't the Turk know the victor's language?"[7]

They are there, in Montenegro, some of them Picasso's friends. Indeed, an international brigade of volunteers has collected, from Milan, Paris, Vienna, Rome, Saint Petersburg. Their accents join these reports as well.

Whose voice is Picasso flagging when he lets the Tchataldja dateline surge forth from beneath the bridge of his otherwise stately violin? The assumption on the part of the scholars who analyze "what the papers say" is that for Picasso to cut a fragment from a newspaper—particularly when, by respecting the columnar layout, the piece allows itself to be read—is for him to produce a "statement."[8] Even if it is through the voices of others, Picasso is assumed to be speaking here. And if Picasso is speaking, we should listen; for aren't these his beliefs?

• • •

At first they seem to circulate through the crystal air like so many weightless facets, the lights struck off a revolving but invisible chandelier. Their glinting meanings—now this, now that—play in the register of the visible the way Mallarmé's notorious homophonies play in the field of the audible: *cygne* or *signe*? *naître* or *n'être*? *verre* or *vers*? *blanc* (white) or *blanc* (blank)?* And even Picasso's fascination with the turned fragment—one the back of the other's front—seems to lead in

---

*The homophonic series that Derrida suspends as a single "title" over his essay "The Double Session"—"L'antre de Mallarmé," "L'entre de Mallarmé," and "L'entre-deux 'Mallarmé' " ("The 'Into' of Mallarmé," "The 'Inter' of Mallarmé," "The Antre of Mallarmé," and "The In-two of 'Mallarmé' ")—is compared by him to Mallarmé's idea of a *lustre*, or crystal chandelier, hanging over a stage. This image of the *lustre* (because the internal replication of its facets reflecting into one another makes it a mirror into which no reality outside it is reflected) will function emblematically as Derrida develops not only the idea of a kind of mimicry that mimes nothing—being what Mallarmé calls "a perpetual allusion without breaking the mirror"—but a structural condition of the fold and the "re-mark," which he will call "dissemination." As the present chapter moves the semiotic system of collage closer and closer to this idea of fold and re-mark (see pp. 78, 81), the emblem of the *lustre* will become increasingly important. See Jacques Derrida, "The Double Session" (1970), in *Dissemination*, trans. Barbara Johnson [Chicago: University of Chicago Press, 1981], 173–285; for analysis of the fold as re-mark, see 251–58.

the direction of Mallarmé's "fold," the sacred cleft of the book's binding, where one page closes over another in sensuous duplicity.

Almost from the very outset of this series of collages, executed so minimally, so sparely, with just news clippings, charcoal, and the white of the drafting paper, Picasso had evoked Mallarmé (Fig. 4). He had cut a headline from a page of *Le Journal* so as to read "Un coup de thé . . . ," signaling for his group of poet friends, the innermost circle of the *band à Picasso*, the title of Mallarmé's most notorious work, "Un coup de dés."[9] Sprinkling the lines of type upon the page, some large but truncated, some a kind of middle voice insistently rising into one's perceptual field, the rest a tiny scatter of type, he could have imagined he was performing the poem's arabesquelike refusal of the regular poetic stanza with its docile block of gray. Just as, in turning the twin of the "Tchataldja" clipping over on its back, he could see himself entering into the logic of the "fold," the logic of the facet, the logic of the binary in which as the sign circulates it constantly reattaches itself to meaning: *cygne/signe*, white/black.

The game of the fold is almost nowhere played more cunningly than in a pair of collages, twinned at the level of the charcoal drawing—which sparely designates the neck and throat of a bottle, the curve of a supporting table, and a series of other highly schematic lines, some gridlike, some diagonal (Figs. 2 and 3). In both collages the bottle "itself" consists of a vertical axis that terminates in a circle we inevitably read as the disc of the vessel's base. But in the one case, the axis is articulated through a column of newsprint pasted onto the white page, with the circle cut out of its lower flange. In the other, which is executed on a full page of newspaper, the same vertical axis-plus-excised-circle has been scissored out of white paper, obliterating the newsprint ground and reminding us of the ultimate backing for the collage in the white of the supporting sheet.

There have been various passes at reading one or another of these collages in ways that slow the circulation of the signifiers to a stop and supply a single signified for the newsprint column. Either understood as standing for the bottle itself or for its liquid contents, this identification then expands to include the textual content of the news clipping and thereby to produce an ideologically expanded interpretation: this is "the stuff on which French culture is temporarily drunk," it concludes.[10] And needless to say, the fact that the support for one member of this pair of collages is the financial page of *Le Journal* reinforces this sense of what Picasso's ideological project must be.

But Picasso's collage piece (in either its positive or its negative—cut-out—guise) is not simply columnar. It is an elongated L from which a circle has been removed. Thus the short arm of the L extends beyond what could be imagined as the perimeter of the object, to suggest itself as the bottle's cast shadow. Since the vertical axis that defines the long arm of the L's left-hand edge extends up into the object's throat, this axial line further proposes itself as a center around which the fin of paper might rotate in order to describe the cylindrical volume of the object. (This suggestion of a rotating fin is even stronger in the collage executed on the financial page, since a second fin, in black, its upper edge cut on a slant, abuts the first, hinting at foreshortening.) Like the paired *f*s that inscribe *depth* or *turning* onto a frontal plane, this extremely economic shape—an L from which a circular notch has been cut—becomes the signifier of an axis slicing into the sheet itself to open its bidimensionality to the experience of a page turning. Front to back, around a central spine. The impossible fold it writes onto the collage sheet inscribes both something like the memory of the volume of a bottle and something like the feeling of the space that would contain it. And if the fold is something like a page turning, it is a page—and this is to be explained presently—taken out of Mallarmé . . .

. . . But then the voices begin. The one that speaks from the very ground of this work pronounces *Le Journal*'s weekly roundup of financial news: "La semaine économique & financière." It gives the stock exchange report under the rubric "Coulisse." It speaks about the upcoming London conference to negotiate the armistice in the Balkans. In these last weeks of November and throughout December, the period in which Picasso is making this first great series of collages, it is indeed of the armistice that most of the voices telling Balkan stories speak, whether or not from the point of view of Montenegro's King Nicolas.

For of course the problem is, who is speaking? And on whose behalf?

The most ardent reader/interpreter of these newspaper

texts is positive that it is Picasso who is speaking here, if not with his own voice, then through the vehicle of these reports. "Picasso juxtaposed readable columns of newsprint," writes Patricia Leighten, "whose authors insistently reiterated subjects of specific concern to left-wing radicals: war, war profiteers, machinating politicians, ministerial abuses of power, strikes and strike-breaking, anarchist and pacifist antiwar demonstrations. The news items accumulate to project an image of French politics as venal, power-mongering, and posing a crazy threat to all those values of humanity and civilization that Picasso's work had always embraced." In using the financial page to make his statement, Picasso, says Leighten, is employing the stock market's reaction to the war news to meditate on the effects of capitalism: "While some profit from war, others suffer disastrously. Thus this collage affirms the direct link between war and the economic health of nations. That the isolated bottle seems to rest on a table formed by the newspaper itself suggests that the economic structure making café life possible rests on the uncertain and despotic whimsy of uncontrollable world events."[11]

Thus we are told that here, in the collage called *Bottle on a Table*, it is Picasso who is speaking. It is his "exploration of these politicized themes" we encounter, his "thoughts" we read, his "criticism" that is "offered."[12]

Without entering into the debate about how much of these texts a viewer of the collages might have been imagined to read—the title of the paper with its play on *Le Journal*, variously cut into JOU or JOUR or URNAL? the big headlines like

"Un Coup de Thé . . ."? the subheads? the fine type?[13]—and without arguing whether their projected audience was to have been a large circle of friends or a restricted audience of two (Braque and Gris)[14] or only the lone reader in the person of their maker, we need to acknowledge that textual fragments join with the other signifiers in these collages and circulate along with them. And without actually reading the stories embedded in its ground, we see plainly that one of the *Bottle on a Table* collages sits astride the title announcing "The Week of Economic and Financial News." A voice we have no difficulty taking note of, sounding as it does at the scale of a headline. And yet, we are still entitled to ask, is it Picasso's?

• • •

At first they cycle through the system of the collage, each fragment in constant semantic play. A trapezoid of newsprint generates the silhouette of a wine glass; another fragment, a cascade of repeated curves, conjures up the complicated form of a bottle, deceptively labeled SUZE (Fig. 5). Pasted on an oval of bright blue paper, the newsprint fragments activate this ground in different ways, the former—tan wedge against blue field—declaring it the solid surface of a table top, the latter, through figure/ground reversal triggered by the rhyme of echoing curves, lifting the selfsame blue off the "table plane" to produce it as the *transparency* of the bottle's surface. And around this visually complex oval center, even more bands of newsprint fan open like the cards in a triumphant player's hand. The airiness of this "space" that surrounds the table with its glass and bottle, and its shifting shadows, is unmistakable . . .

. . . And yet from the very bottom of the space's edge a headline obtrudes. "Les Serbes s'avancent . . ." ("The Serbs Advance"), it says; and this "atmosphere" fills with voices. To the table's left is a news clipping reporting on a pacifist meeting attended by fifty thousand people and addressed by a variety of left-wing speakers, from the parliament member Marcel Sembat to the German socialist Scheidemann, calling for French and German workers not to fire on one another in "a general European war" or to die "for the capitalists and the manufacturers of arms and munitions." The right-hand splay of columns is the "Walk on the Battlefield," with a report of cholera that has devastated the Turkish soldiers, this account pasted upside down on the page. Below the table, with the dateline "16 November," is news of the Serbian advance toward Monastir in Macedonia and the siege against Adrianople. Only the ripple of print from within the bottle's multiple perimeters speaks in a different tone: it is a fragment from a serial novel satirizing upper-class rakes.

This collage, *Glass and Bottle of Suze*, has been characterized as the representation of a conversation taking place around a café table: the discussion of Picasso and his friends, talking politics and pacifism and war. But more than this, these selections, it is said, give us Picasso's own position, not only on "these issues," which "Picasso explored through 'quoting' with the newsprints he selected," but on the very issue of the newspaper itself, the vehicle of information through which the "news" must inevitably pass.[15] The newspaper, the argument goes, is systematized distraction, politics and fashion, sports and advertising abutting one another in a kaleidoscope of topics, each its own seemingly independent segment. It is this very randomness and disarray that seems to stand for, to be the warrant of, the "objectivity" of the news itself, its beholdenness to no interest, to no voice. But disarray, in the newspaper, has its own work to do, which is to disorganize the space of narrative and of history and of memory and to sell news instead as distraction. The commodification of news is the newspaper's business, and it isn't just confined to the printed ads. Instead, it is disjunction itself that does the work of advertising, turning news into entertainment, history into spectacle, memory into commodity.

This transformative ability, the argument continues, ultimately projects the force of the centralized, dominant voice of power in modern Western societies, a voice that deceptively masks its message behind the motley of all the different sections and headlines of the newspaper's separate rubrics, creating thereby a jumble that "neutralizes what would otherwise be their cumulative and interconnected logic: they systematically 'rationalize disjunction; they are organized *as disorganization*.' "[16] But Picasso, it is argued, sees through this cacophony to its purely venal, commercialized core and his response is to shape these bits and pieces into an organized montage: "Picasso structures the collage through juxtaposition in a way that reconceptualizes and transforms both the pictorial system and the commodified character of the daily paper." Here are voices that jump past the barriers of the newspaper's dispersal to be brought together in such a way as to produce its author's own critique, for, if in the dominant form of the newspaper the voices are fragmented, "in the collage, Picasso has created the potential for a narrative by juxtaposing this satirical novel on a libertine aristocracy with grisly stories from the Balkan War and reports of a mobilized left-wing. Moreover, he has done it in a Cubist style whose assumed 'anti-aesthetic,' 'anti-French' disorderliness was aligned to anarchism in the critical press."[17]

The argument that is presented here claims to derive from Mikail Bakhtin. Bakhtin's analysis of the voice of power as it speaks through "dominant discourse," of which the mass-circulation newspaper is one prime example, is summoned as a way of understanding what is seen as Picasso's strategy to produce a "counter-discourse" and thus to rebind what the centralizing power of the dominant culture has seen fit to dissever.

Yet to read any page of Bakhtin's own dazzling account of the work of Dostoevsky, in which the novelist's relation to journalism is also exploited to forge the "fundamentally new novelistic genre" of the polyphonic novel, is both to find striking parallels with Picasso's invention in these collages and to encounter a repeated critique of the argument I have just been summarizing, an argument that Bakhtin would have seen as "re-monologizing" these works and thereby masking the "radical artistic revolution" (Bakhtin's words) that is at stake.

Defining Dostoevsky's polyphony as "*a plurality of indepen-*

dent and unmerged voices and consciousnesses" and making this the chief characteristic of his radical poetics, Bakhtin argues: "What unfolds in his works is not a multitude of characters and fates in a single objective world, illuminated by a single authorial consciousness; rather a *plurality of consciousnesses, with equal rights and each with its own world*, combine but are not merged in the unity of the event."[18]

Again and again, Bakhtin rehearses the various analyses of Dostoevsky's work offered by literary critics whom Bakhtin respects, many of whom focus on the fabric of conversation and argument from which these novels are woven, making them multivoiced and multileveled, or polyphonic. But again and again, Bakhtin shows that the admission of this presence of polyphony, or of what he also calls "dialogism," is made only to be taken back again, insofar as these multiple voices are resynthesized by these critics into the old, traditional, monological form. In general, there are two ways of doing this. One is to take the polyphony present in the novels as a reflection of the multivoicedness found in the real world and thus to "transfer [one's] explanations directly from the plane of the novel to the plane of reality." The effect of doing this, Bakhtin says, is to characterize the novel as a single consciousness's vision of this fragmented world, something that is quite the contrary of Dostoevsky's procedure. For if "the monologic unity of the world is destroyed in a Dostoevsky novel . . . those ripped-off pieces of reality are in no sense directly combined in the unity of the novel: each of these pieces gravitates toward the integral field of vision of a specific character;

each makes sense only at the level of a specific consciousness." Thus Bakhtin's critique is that, "if these chunks of reality deprived of any pragmatic links were combined directly as things emotionally, lyrically, or symbolically harmonious in the unity of a single and monologic field of vision, then before us would be the world of the Romantics, the world of Hoffmann, for example, but in no way could it be Dostoevsky's world" (20–21).

In our Picasso example of the *Suze* collage, this option would be the one of seeing the work as a represented conversation taking place around a café table. Someone (Picasso) is observing a dialogue taking place in all the fragmented multiplicity of how it happens in the real world, but it is his "monologic field of vision" that brings it to us.

The second tendency in remonologizing Dostoevsky's dialogical invention, Bakhtin says, is to understand the constant voicing of different positions as part of an ideological project and to try to identify which of these ideas are Dostoevsky's own. (The parallel with the *Suze* interpretation would be to see the collage as projecting Picasso's putative idea of counterdiscourse.) This again is to remonologize the novels by making them either the expression of a single consciousness (the author's) or the reflection of a dialectical progression of the idea. Synthesized into the evolution of a unified spirit then, "each novel would form a completed philosophical whole, structured according to the dialectical method. We would have in the best instance a philosophical novel, a novel with an idea . . . [or] in the worst instance we would have philosophy in the form of a novel." But in Dostoevsky we have neither. Dostoevsky, Bakhtin writes, "doesn't represent the 'idea in itself' (Plato), nor the 'ideal existence' as phenomenologists understand it. For Dostoevsky no ideas, thoughts, positions exist 'in themselves' belonging to no one." And this is because "the idea is not the hero of his novels, but a man. The idea for him was either a touchstone for testing the man in man, or a form for revealing it, or a 'medium,' an environment in which human consciousness could be revealed in its deepest essence" (25–26).

That essence, as we know, is conflictual. It is in constant argument both with itself and with others. Every thought is thus "accompanied by a continual sideways glance at another person." Every thought "senses itself to be from the very beginning a *rejoinder* in an unfinalized dialogue. Such thought," Bakhtin explains again and again, "is not impelled toward a well-rounded, finalized, systemically monologic whole. It lives a tense life on the borders of someone else's thought" (32).

This conflictual character not only produces the internalized drama of contradictions within a single character, "forcing a character to converse with his own double," but also leads Dostoevsky to invent dialogically paired characters, coupled opponents (like Ivan and the Devil, Raskolnikov and Svidrigailov, etc.) who become a way of "dramatizing the contradictions within one person" (28). And indeed it is this doubling, this opening up of an oppositional pair on the site of every supposed unity, that constitutes Dostoevsky's formal strength: "Where others saw a single thought, he was able to find and feel out two thoughts, a bifurcation; where others saw a single quality, he discovered in it the presence of a second and contradictory quality. Everything that seemed simple became, in his world, complex and multi-structured. In every voice he could hear two contending voices" (30).

And it is this dialogism lying at the heart of Dostoevsky's poetics that is to be found as well in the newspapers to which the author contributed in his guise as journalist. While Bakhtin has no interest in Dostoevsky's biography as an explanatory fulcrum for his analysis, this journalistic practice, which requires that everything be treated in the context of the present and that issues of causality be constantly suspended, is not unconnected to Dostoevsky's invention: "His love of the newspaper, his deep and subtle understanding of the newspaper page as a living reflection of the contradictions of contemporary society in the cross-section of a single day, where the most diverse and contradictory material is laid out, extensively, side by side and one side against the other," is not an explanation for Dostoevsky's artistic vision, but rather is itself explained by that vision (29).

The polyphony that Bakhtin sees in Dostoevsky, the opening of an oppositional pair on the very site of every identity supposed as singular, is what we have seen happen in what I have been characterizing as Picasso's circulation of the sign. And this whirl of signifiers reforming in relation to each other and reorganizing their meanings seemingly out of nothing, in an almost magical disjunction from reality, this manipulation at the level of structure, can also be appreciated—and once again the parallel with Dostoevsky is welcome—at the level of the textual representation of the "voice." Each voice, in dialogue at least with itself, is doubled and dramatized by becoming the voice of another.

For, whoever is speaking of capitalist exploitation through Picasso's repeated use of the market reports, either in the form of the complete financial page as in *Bottle on a Table* or in smaller, more fragmented doses (Figs. 7, 10), another, quite different voice—possibly Apollinaire's—is also speaking on behalf of fraudulence and *blague* (trickery). Who could forget the hilarious spectacle of Apollinaire posing as a market expert and offering stock tips to the American poet Stuart Merrill on the basis of his position as editor of a half-phony financial magazine? As many others joined in asking his advice on investments, André Salmon and other of Apollinaire's close friends watched these performances, knowing how "totally ignorant he was of every aspect of the Bourse."[19] But, then, the fabrication of information was as natural to Apollinaire as breathing.

• • •

At first they seem to turn through the limpid space like so many glinting facets on the surface of water. The newspaper fragments on both of them date from early December, one a *Siphon, Glass, Newspaper, Violin* (Fig. 6), the other a *Bowl with Fruit, Violin and Wineglass* (Fig. 7).

The first has the stark simplicity of the "Tchataldja" *Violin,* just a few shards of newsprint, plus a fragment of wood-grained wallpaper, pasted to the white page articulated here and there by spare charcoal lines. The title "JOURNAL" excised from the newspaper itself is attached to a drawn oblong as its unambiguous label. A swatch of ads scissored into the shape of a seltzer bottle, its lines of type upended, releases the lettering within the perimeters of the "siphon" into the sign for rising bubbles. Another piece of newsprint produces the stippled atmospheric *space* to cup the neck of the violin. A fourth patch is the operator of the work's complexity as its prismatic contour manages to function as both *figure* and *ground*; its shape mimicking that of the wineglass Picasso has drawn onto its surface and, by simultaneously serving to profile the violin's left shoulder, executing a figure/ground reversal that propels it backward to signify the light-filled surround for all these objects.

Bowl with Fruit takes this production of the oppositional pair from within the supposed unity of the single collage piece and expands it over the surface of the entire work. The wood-grained paper cut to the profile of the violin extends past the instrument to insinuate itself as the ground of the table that supports the compote dish, signaling at one and the same time *figure* and *ground*.[20] The black rectangle that elongates the blue plane of the violin's face to produce the solid *opacity* of its neck is also coerced by an abutting white shape to read as the *transparency* of shadow. Even the page from a commercial illustration of fruit types is forced into this play of the double, since each element gathered into the concavity of the "bowl" is a naturalistic rendering of apple or pear (figure) appearing against the white of the page (background); and yet, cut into a set of paper shards—trapezoids, rhomboids, rectangles—that literally overlap one another in their pasted configuration, each of these white grounds opacifies to become a *figure*, each paper shape obstructing the view of its neighbor . . .

. . . But in both these works the sound of voices bubbles to the surface. In the former the legible type within the siphon initiates the talk, with a "proposition intéressante" ("good deal") concerning "vêtements confectionnés" ("ready-made clothes"), followed by the sputter of "prêt," "prêt," "prêt," "prêts" ("loans") from the adjoining classified ads. In the other the headline for "La Vie Sportive" ("The Sporting Life") pits the racing news against ". . . arition," the title of a story about a séance ("Apparition") where a Madame Harmelie encounters the departed spirit of her desire ("C'est elle!" ["That's her!"]). Whoever chooses to read the fine print will go on to other topics: a medical case history detailing the patient's muscle tone and the amounts of morphine administered, the stock data given in the "Chronique Financière," an adman's assurances about the powers of a certain brand of motor oil.

So many voices let into the space, each with its world, its tone, its point of view.

It is like Apollinaire's conversation poem "Les Fenêtres" ("Windows"), also written in December, where the voices are unnamed although recognizable to the poet's friends. Apollinaire himself starts the talk off with the announcement

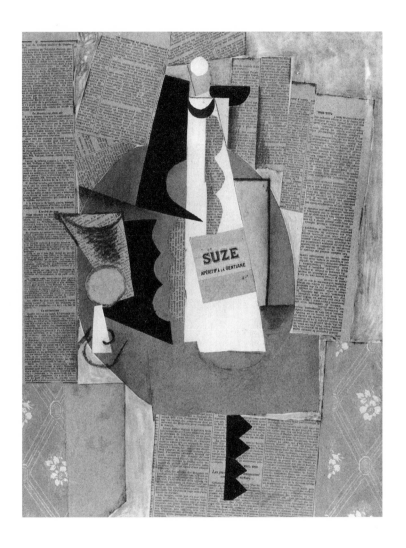

5.

Glass and Bottle of Suze

autumn 1912

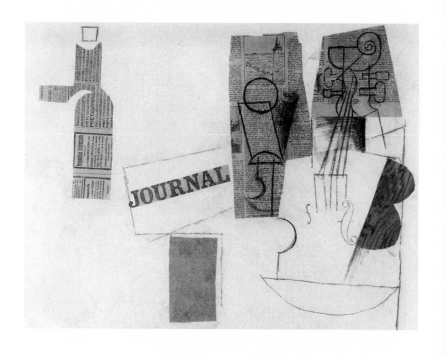

6.
Siphon, Glass, Newspaper, Violin
autumn–winter 1912

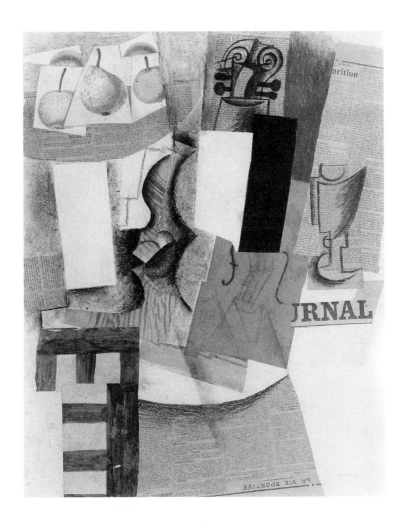

7.

Bowl with Fruit, Violin and Wineglass

autumn–winter 1912

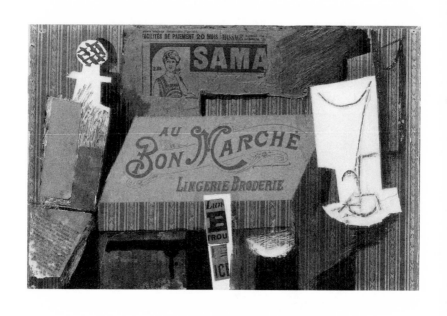

8.
Still-life "Au Bon Marché"
early 1913

that "From red to green the yellow dies entirely," but some-one else replies, "There's a poem to write about the bird with one wing," and a third asks someone to "Raise the blind." "We'll send it by telegraph," suggests a fourth. Each of these fragments is just enough to produce the motion of conver-sation, the play of relations, the sociability of the group. None is enough to solidify into "information" or "argument" or "idea." And none can be said to represent the position of the author of "Les Fenêtres," not even the title, which is Delau-nay's.[21]

It is this aspect of conversation that Picasso stages in these collages. Whatever he might have felt about the politics of the newspaper's layout—either Mallarmé's disgust or Dos-toevsky's pleasure—or about the contents of the texts, it seems undeniable that the printed type acts so as to parallel and re-double the activity of the visual forms. For if in the latter the signs offer just enough visual support for the circulation of meaning, in the former there is just enough meaning—in the form of the voices, in the guise of the "news" they utter—to support the circulation of the sign: to float the bits and pieces of text in a circuit that could be defined as more abstract than Bakhtin's dialogism, for it is conversation understood as the almost disembodied matrix that the sociologist Georg Simmel would define as the categorical precondition of sociability it-self.

• • •

At first they seem to fan through the brilliance of the room like moving shadows cast from an unseen source, perhaps branches waving outside the window, so that now it's the dark that makes the pattern, now it's the light one watches. In *Still-life "Au Bon Marché"* (Fig. 8) the snap of white on black plays a particular game of over and under since what seems to be incised out of the wallpaper surface, indeed what is even labeled "TROU, ICI" ("hole, here"), is in fact a buildup of very shallow relief, like a thin slab of gesso hovering above the patterned ground.

The irony of the increased material presence of what has been declared to be an absence, a lacuna, contributes to the ambiguity that settles into the lower center of the image. Executed entirely on the top of one of the department store's cardboard boxes, the collage exploits the box top's label— "Au Bon Marché, Lingerie, Broderie"—the form of which (a parallelogram) allows it to be flipped, with a little help from Picasso, into perspective so that it will itself appear as the top of a box nestled within a decorative setting of ornamental stripes that come to stand for "wallpaper."[22] The help Picasso provides is in the introduction of a shadowy wash that projects a front face and right-hand side for this "box," even while maintaining (*Bowl of Fruit*–style) the utter continuity of the striped surface that now functions as both figure and ground. Because of this continuous flow, the extent of the box is unclear. The articulation of the front façade plus the label identifying it as "Lingerie Broderie" suggest that it is a shallow traylike container, while the elongation of the right-hand side almost to the bottom edge of the work implies with equal plausibility that the object in question is a deep coffer, more like a locked casket.

Should it be the latter, the "hole" referred to would signal the lock of this box and thus obliterate the kind of space Picasso often suggests as circulating below the table top of the collage still lifes—in *Bowl with Fruit*, for example, or *Bottle of Suze*. Should it be the former, then the lock functions, as it had in analytic cubist paintings such as *The Dressing Table* (1910), as the keyhole in the drawer below the table surface, which, whatever its symbolic function, also serves as an admission (operational since Cézanne's early still lifes) that for a painting, the place where the table hangs suspended several inches above the lower framing edge is always a vexatious visual "hole" indeed.[23] The shadows cast from the decanter on the left (whose cut-glass stopper also suggests that it might be a bottle of perfume) or the goblet on the right, reinforcing the sense of a table plane, offer no further help in this matter. All that seems certain is that we are in a decidedly feminine space, a boudoir with its dressing table, and that on the wall above this assemblage of objects appears the kind of array of feminine pictures so often found there, indicated here by the ad Picasso has appropriated from the Samaritaine department store but cut now to read only "SAMA" next to the image of a young woman wearing a lace bodice and adjusting her necklace.

The boudoir, the lace, the cut-glass flask, the casket—all suggest a presence that had inflected these collages before in the direction of poetry but does so now in a bow toward fashion. We seem to hear the tones of Mallarmé, writing in *La dernière mode* under the pen name Ix. "Let such a volume [of verse] linger for eight days, half-opened, like a bottle of scent," he advises, "on silk cushions embroidered with fantasies; and let that other volume [of tales] pass from this testing ground onto the lacquered surface of a heavy cabinet—jewel boxes near at hand, locked shut until the next party," for Ix assumes his reader to be a woman.[24] Or, in yet another of his personae, that of Miss Satin, who signs the magazine's "Fashion" column, he admits: "We have all dreamt of this gown, without knowing it. Monsieur Worth, alone, knew how to create a *toilette* as elusive as our thoughts." This is Mallarmé who, indeed, considers each detail of a dress, and each detail of its description, as "the thousand charming nothings" designed to imply less the physicality of an objective presence before him than a magical, evanescent, global effect. An effect not unlike the one he called for in poetry.

Within his magazine *La dernière mode*, Mallarmé spun a multitude of voices out of his own, giving each a different column to write, a different world to represent. Not only was there Ix, who covered literature and the theater, or Miss Satin, who commented on *le high-life*; Marguerite de Ponty addressed "Fashion," the "Chef de bouche de chez Brabant" published elegant menus, Marliani advised on interior decoration in the column called the "Carnet d'or," for which Zizi, the mulatto maid, also supplied a recipe for coconut jam. Mallarmé held this sparkling conversation with himself throughout the fall of 1874, a conversation he took so seriously that ten years later, when Verlaine asked him for an autobiographical note for a kind of "Who's Who" of France, he ended his self-description with *La dernière mode*, "the eight or ten published issues of which inspire me still, when I groom them of their dust, to dream on at length."[25]

But other dreams besides the ideal of these dematerialized "nothings" find their voice in Picasso's *"Au Bon Marché."* Indeed, the allusion to the white sale (B is for BLANC), to the trousseau (the "hole" of the truncated TROU from the ad is a reference to this), to the precious horde of undergarments, is uttered as well in the tone of the *midinette* whose shopgirl's sensibility, quite the opposite of Ix's or Marguerite de Ponty's, is formed on the packaged sentimentality of serial novels such as *Le Journal*'s *roman-feuilletons* ("You know, Miss Jodel, that if ever you need my help . . ." —"Too late!"),[26] the belief in spiritualism ("C'est elle!"), the emotions of dance tunes such as "Trilles et Baisers" ("Trills and Kisses" [Daix, 518, 521]), and, most of all, the vicarious thrill of the *fait-divers*. The *fait-divers*, which is news reduced to gossip, information making its way more or less in the form of rumor, is a kind of false coin put in mass circulation by the newspaper and read with avidity by the concièrge, the dressmaker's assistant, and—by her own admission—Picasso's Fernande Olivier, the great consumer of sensationalism, *romans à l'eau de rose*, and playlets of personal tragedy. Fernande, who, kidnapped, raped, and held prisoner as a sixteen-year-old by the young man her aunt will then force her to marry, loses herself in magazines: "I am left alone the whole day; I can't leave. I found a pile of illustrated *Gil Blas* that I devour without dreaming of nourishing myself physically. When the evening comes, I am there, crouched on the sofa with the magazines scattered around me. I have forgotten about time, about life. These poems, these stories, these songs, these pictures, how full of talent this Steinlen is!"[27]

This is Fernande, who at the age of seventy-four composed a fraudulent "diary" of her adolescence and her subsequent career as artist's model, widely shared sexual object, and mistress: fraudulent—since it is clearly no diary—and filled not only with "biographical" details surely modeled on years of romance reading but with embarrassing attempts at literary style that constantly fall back into purple prose:

I love the radishes I unearth, the sorrel leaves that set one's teeth on edge, I love—like the Parisian I am—everything that country children disdain. I love that summer thunderstorms catch me by surprise to make me a dripping thing with hair streaming onto my neck, I love to feel the water slipping between my skin and my slip and not be able to move forward since my dress, glued to my body, impedes my legs, and to feel my face glistening with rain, the water in my eyes, my ears, down my neck, and then, the rain stopping, a rainbow streaking the repurified azure, lets me slide on the sparkling grass and feel myself dry under the burning rays of the sun, restored to itself again.[28]

It is the document of a mind nurtured on pulp romance, in which the cliché of the prostitute—indolent, gluttonous, lesbian—able to rise in society and be made whole again by the noble intervention of a painter (the examples here are a *roman-feuilleton* like Xavier de Montepin's *La porteuse de pain* or the extraordinary *Mémoires* of Céleste Mogador, a registered prostitute in the 1840s who became a countess by 1854[29]) mixes with the middle-class idealization of art.

Two stories touching on Fernande are told by Gertrude Stein through the voice of Alice Toklas. The first—addressing Fernande's literary tastes—is the jealousy she exhibited during her separation from Picasso in 1907, upon finding out that it was Picasso to whom Stein had given the month's supply of "funnies" from American newspapers. The second is Picasso's comment—straight out of "Un amour de Swann"—after his definitive separation from her in 1911: "He said her beauty always held him but he could not stand any of her little ways."[30] Indeed, both Salmon and Sabartès speak pityingly of "Picasso's eight years of boredom."[31]

And indeed, the shopgirl who speaks in *"Au Bon Marché"* has, herself, two "voices." The first, calling to mind Fernande's demand for a maid and a "day" (to receive regularly) after she and Picasso had moved to the boulevard de Clichy in 1911, is drenched in propriety. She shops the white sales. She thinks about her trousseau, her undergarments. But the second is pictured by Octave Uzanne, writing a sociology of Parisian women in 1910 and describing the young middle-class girl taught from the age of fifteen to think about nothing but love and flirtation, who then marries into coldness and boredom but lives "in a city overflowing with sexual excitement."[32] How could there not be scandal? he asks. These are the women who exploit the classified ads of the newspapers and, under the guise of offering "massages, hair removal, dye jobs," make sexual contacts.[33] Thus in *"Au Bon Marché,"* above the Samaritaine ad, Picasso includes a thin strip of the classifieds with MASSAGE a prominent offering, and even more nastily he has "trousseau" play associations with "trou"—as in Apollinaire's early pornographic novel *Mirely, or The Little Low-Priced Hole.*

If the circulation of the sign is shadowed by the circulation of news, of rumor, of commercial offerings of various kinds, all of them given "voice" by these surges of type, one of the speakers here is talking sex for money, while another (the same?) is dreaming of romance, and yet another is musing on fashion and its expressive form, coquetry.

Thinking about the distance between these two—coquetry and prostitution—in 1910, just a few years before Picasso made this collage, Georg Simmel sees them both as a form of abstraction.[34] But whereas prostitution strips both seller and buyer of his or her subjectivity, reducing each to nothing but a pure means for the denuded sex act, in which the organ is given an equivalent in money with no remainder (indeed, the economic counterpart of the prostitutional relation *is* money), coquetry, he argues, is something else altogether. There, as the coquette manages to hold her pursuer in constant tension, suspended between her "yes" and her "no," her refusal never produced as an ultimate rebuff, eroticism is stripped of its means/ends content, to become a pure form of play. "This freedom from all the weight of firm content and residual reality," Simmel writes, "gives coquetry that character of vacillation, of distance, of the ideal, which allows one to speak with some right of the 'art'—not the arts—of coquetry."[35]

Coquetry is, then, the aesthetics of sex. It is eroticism as purposiveness without purpose, carnal knowledge stripped of concepts, a Kantian ground of freedom. As this kind of "play form" of eroticism, Simmel compares it to conversation, which is for him the ultimate play form of social relations: pure circulation stripped of all function except that of being the very expression of sociability itself.

To read Simmel's 1910 essay on "Sociability" is to encounter a strange gloss on Picasso's collages of 1912 or Apollinaire's contemporaneous forays into a poetry of "conversation." For Simmel wants to project a social space in which signs circulate endlessly as weightless fragments of repartee, stripped of practical content—that of information, argument, business—taking as their content, instead, the functional play of conversation itself, conversation whose playfulness is expressed by the speed and lightness with which its object changes from moment to moment, giving its topics an interchangeable, accidental character. It is in this way, Simmel says, that conversation is "the purest and most sublimated form of mutuality among all sociological phenomena," since conversation "becomes the most adequate fulfillment of a relation, which is, so to speak, nothing but relationship, in which even that which is otherwise the pure form of inter-action is its own self-sufficient content" (137).

In the art of conversation, Simmel adds, the storyteller con-tributes his or her gift to the social group by telling it imper-sonally so as not to impose an individualized presence—which Simmel calls "the light and shadow of one's inner life"—but instead to enjoy "the impersonal freedom of the mask" (131). The disembodied voice, a pure persona without the three-dimensionality of personhood, thus refuses to make speech the instrument for ulterior ends, emitting it rather as "the abstraction of association," the "whole meaning and content of social processes," and ultimately, since the ideal of conversation is that it should circulate among equals, "the play-form for the ethical forces of concrete society" (139).

It was with this same "tact" that Fénéon sent his "news in three lines" every morning into the whirl of daily circulation, the *fait-divers* as amusing deadpan, the frisson of the almost meaningless event. And Picasso also contributes: "Mr. Char-don's suicide remains mysterious" (Daix 553); "A sixty-year-old is beaten by a burglar and left for dead" (Daix 546); "An actress kills her lover" (Fig. 9). Too fragmented to body forth the dialogical novel's world, they enact the pure circulation of sociability itself, the play form of the not yet fully voiced "statement."

• • •

At first they seem to flutter through the empty space, to land weightlessly on the abstract surface, yellowed leaves blown by the wind, some upside down, some right side up. The play is always most brilliant when the reversals are pairs, as in the *Bottle of Vieux Marc, Glass, and Newspaper* (1913), where a toquelike shape, cut from a sheet of wallpaper, reads as *transparency* by articulating both the lip of the wineglass and its liquid contents, while below, the upside-down silhouette left by the "toque's" excision from the sheet registers the *opacity* of the stem and base of the object, declaring itself a figure (no matter how ghostly) against the wallpaper's tablecloth ground (Fig. 9). The paradigm is perfectly expressed, as the signifiers—identical in shape—produce each other's meaning, their opposition in space (right side up/upside down) echoing their semantic reversal.

In an example from the opening series of these collages during the fall of 1912—the ones reduced to the "ascetic" components of just one or two newspaper pieces against the cursive lines of charcoal on paper—a lone fragment, pasted upside down, holds the center of the work (Fig. 10).[36] It would seem not enough to produce the play-of-the-signifier necessary to these collages, not sufficient to keep the simple iconic, or naturalistic reading at bay. Indeed, Daix says quite flatly, "This cutting expresses the volume of the bottle"; and Rosenblum, having remarked that the lightbulb advertisement that appears on the fragment can be read as a comment on the orientation of the fragment itself ("the only [bulb] which can be placed in any position at all"), goes on to declare that the illustration of the bulb, falling where it does in the center of the work, "transforms this bottle-shaped volume into a lamp base (with arced shade), yet another example of Cubist sleight of hand."[37]

The pressure to turn the collage-sign back into an icon with a purely mimetic thrust is very like the pressure Bakhtin speaks of, even while resisting it, to remonologize the space of Dostoevsky's polyphony. Daix's impulse is that of simplifying—"It's the volume of the bottle"—whereas the trapezoid of the clipping, set within a cursively drawn oblong, from the upper edge of which another, narrower rectangle rises, with the indication of the neck of the bottle jutting from its top edge, renders perfectly ambiguous the identity of these objects and the relation between them. Insofar as the block of advertising on the clipping can be read as a label, the newsprint seems to articulate the wine bottle (much in the style of a somewhat later, rather similar member of the series [Daix 547] whose sole clipping, an inverted trapezoid, places the ad for "Vin Désiles" at the point where a label would be affixed to its schematic profile of a bottle). But because the oblong to which the newsprint is attached seems to extend beyond the bottle and to rest in front of it, the clipping appears to affix itself to and thereby to signal a third, unnamed element on the table: the daily paper so ubiquitous among the other members of this series. Yet even more important, since the long trapezoidal shape of the newsprint suggests a foreshortened canting into depth, it signifies the *transparency* of the collage system itself, the shuttling relationships between one figure and another (newspaper and bottle) or between figures and their grounds. (In the case of the "Vin Désiles" collage a

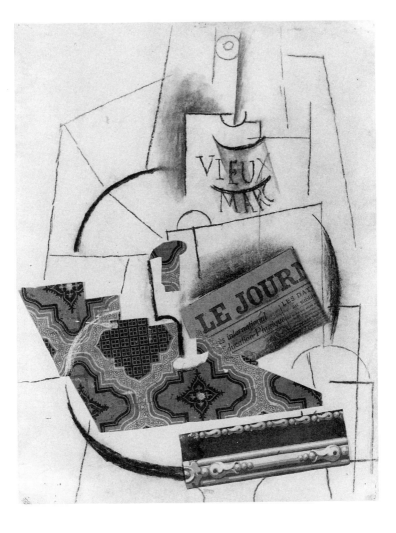

9.

Bottle of Vieux Marc, Glass and Newspaper

spring 1913

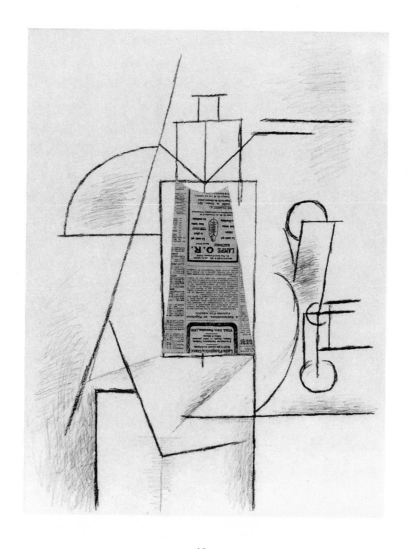

10.
Bottle and Wineglass
autumn–winter 1912

similar ambiguity occurs as the "label," rhyming in shape with the bowl of the wineglass that is sketched in beside it, attaches itself now to the bottle and now to the goblet, alternating as figure and ground.)

If Daix's reading presses this spatial and semantic ambiguity out of the work, it does not violate the collage's representational order. Rosenblum's, on the other hand, pushes toward an iconic condition that is utterly foreign to Picasso's system. The idea that Picasso is "finding" realistic images in the clippings out of which to construct a naturalistic representation— "a lamp base (with arced shade)"—converts this signifying system into a naive game of projection. This does violence to Picasso's evident control over the sign's circulation within a universe of fairly fixed parameters, not only in terms of its repertory of objects and their scale in relation to one another but also in terms of the semes (or units of meaning) the collage pieces will generate. Nowhere is this naturalizing tendency more vulgar than in Edward Fry's reading of *"Au Bon Mar-ché,"* which, taking off from Rosenblum's earlier suggestion that Picasso is punning with the prominent placement of the word *trou*, sees this "hole" as the linchpin of the collage's putative depiction of "a woman of apparently easy virtue" seated behind a café table, her "legs beneath the table [indicated] by clippings with the pun 'LUN B TROU ICI.' "[38] The idea that Picasso would break the tension of the breathless closeup within which he controls these still lifes to open up the deep perspective of a woman behind a table or that he would violate the coherence of scale that is part of his system to build a composite figure with dwarf head and colossal genitals goes against all the other evidence of this entire practice as it evolves from work to work, maintaining the logic of a series . . .

. . . And when the voices begin they refer to other things. The one that emerges from the lightbulb advertisement speaks, as Rosenblum caught, in the tones of a modernist game of self-reference. "The only [bulb] which gives light on all sides," it boasts, from its own upside-down position. And then another voice, which also rises from within this ad, pronounces "LAMPE O.R.," and is reinforced by the fragment Picasso cut from the next day's paper to use on another collage (Fig. 11), in which a voice announces "[LE L] ITRE D'OR" ("The Golden Litre"). Speaking reflexively, then, of the collage piece itself, it is also speaking of gold.

There are many who would say that to refer to the materials of collage and, at one and the same time, to speak of gold, is a contradiction in terms. The very *point* of collage, they would say, its radicality at the level of cultural production, is that these are materials born to die. If high art is addressed to timeless values like beauty or truth, it chisels this speech into the hardness of granite, seeking out those materials, like gold, that time will neither fade nor erode. The method in the artist's choice of oil paint or bronze or marble is one of securing a permanence of form to underwrite a presumed timelessness of content. But paper is the Achilles' heel of the art system, rendered perishable by light, by worms, by mold. And nothing in the entire range of fiber could be more visibly open to attack than the newspaper, yellowing as it does in the course of a week, under one's very eyes.

The defiance of high art, the argument goes, is written into this "pasted paper revolution" most visibly by the use of newsprint, although all the other paper objects—the cigarette packs, the matchbooks, the wallpaper, the department store and bottle labels—flaunt their connection to a mass-cultural source just as openly, thereby shrugging their shoulders at the sacred preserve of high culture and its values.[39] Even the technique of making collage, with its bits and pieces that can be shifted about on the drawing sheet and provisionally pinned in place before their definitive gluing, is derived from commercial practice. It is more reminiscent of layout design than of anything taught at the Ecole des Beaux-Arts.[40]

But Gertrude Stein, turning to the topic of Picasso's collage, has this to report on his notions about ephemerality as defiance:

Later he used to say quite often, paper lasts quite as well as paint and after all if it all ages together why not, and he said further, after all later, no one will see the picture, they will see the legend of the picture, the legend that the picture has created, then it makes no difference if the picture lasts or does not last. Later they will restore it, a picture lives by its legend, not by anything else. He was indifferent as to what might happen to his pictures even though what might happen to them affected him profoundly.[41]

Indeed, without retreating to that "high ground" which would consider nothing but the formal character of collage's operation, other historians, following Stein, insist on weighing the importance of Picasso's own cultural context before assessing the socio-aesthetic meaning of collage. For David Cottington it is simply the case that Picasso—from within the protective shield of a subcultural group that was both internationalist and intensely aestheticist in makeup (composed of collectors, dealers, poets, and a few other artists)—has to be seen as conceiving his collage materials for the same aesthetic ends as obtained for cubism in general, namely, the hermeticism of a symbolist notion of artistic autonomy.[42] So that if these materials seem to speak in the demotic language of dailiness, the point they are making is not to negate the goals of high art but rather, "using means that are within everyone's grasp, [to assert] his power as a creator." Here Cottington is quoting Pierre Daix's position, before going on to generalize what he feels to be the real point Picasso must be making here about the transformative powers, not so much of his own creative gifts as of the aesthetic discourse itself: "turning the dross of the vernacular, as it were, into the gold of art."[43]

Cottington is relatively alone, however, in a chorus of voices that would say "Pish tush!" to a claim that would go so far as to suggest the Mallarméan character of Picasso's collage. They would remind him of Apollinaire's words in "Zone," written just as Picasso was embarking on collage, praising what he saw around him in the streets: "The inscriptions on the sign boards and the walls / The plaques, the notices bawl like parrots." Going even farther, they say, Apollinaire ruptures symbolism's pretty autonomy, its golden isolation from commerce:

> You read the handbills, catalogs, posters that sing out
> loud and clear—
> That's the morning's poetry, and for prose there are
> the newspapers,
> There are tabloids lurid with police reports,
> Portraits of the great and a thousand assorted stories.

"Zone," they would say, was written under the effect of Apollinaire's sudden conversion, in the late spring of 1912, to futurism; hence its embrace of the very medium—journalism and the newspaper—that Mallarmé loathed. Naming Mallarmé the greatest poet of the *nineteenth* century, Marinetti had cried, "Let us reject our symbolist masters!" and Apollinaire was soon to second this in his own poetic manifesto. Given the link between Apollinaire and Picasso, they argue, it is obvious that Picasso's very adoption of newsprint as his work's major support at the outset of collage points to his adherence to the *esprit nouveau* position that understands the world of Mallarmé as irrevocably superseded.[44]

Further, they would add, "Zone" is not merely a celebration of the collapse of the difference between the poetic "high" and the mass-cultural "low." "Zone" has in store another implosion as well. For at the poem's end, the Christianity Apollinaire supports throughout its length is submitted to the challenge of those "fetishes from Oceania and Guinea," which he calls "Christs of darker hopes." Embracing this other "shape and creed," he ends by denigrating the golden, eternal, Western God: "Farewell, farewell," he says, "Decapitated sun—"

So, they retort, the idea of "turning the dross of the vernacular into the gold of art" has to be taken, at this moment, ironically indeed.

And yet . . . it is Picasso who has planted those voices saying "gold"; and as with the case of his proffering of the market reports, we are entitled to ask of these collages: "Who is speaking, and to what end?" For, indeed, even if we take this utterance right at the mass-cultural level of Apollinaire's "tabloids lurid with police reports" or his media "portraits of the great and a thousand assorted stories," we have to admit—and here we would be coming to Cottington's defense in this matter of a Mallarméan Picasso—that it was Mallarmé who composed, something in the manner of Fénéon, a *fait-divers* on the very subject of "gold."

Of the eight essays gathered by Mallarmé under the rubric "Grands Faits Divers," only two—"Or" ("Gold") and "Accusation"—were actually triggered by news stories.[45] The first was stimulated by the financial crash of the Panama Canal venture of Ferdinand de Lesseps, the second by the journalistic accusations against French writers during the wave of anarchist bombings in the 1890s, and more specifically in defense of his friend Laurent Tailhade, whose remark, "Qu'importe la victime si le geste est beau" ("What matter the victim, if the gesture is beautiful"), was distorted by the press.[46] But the "themes" of gold, finance, cash (*numéraire*), and the newspapers themselves are threaded through most of the texts. Indeed, as the Mallarmé scholar Robert Greer Cohn points out, even the title of the de Lesseps piece employs the French word *or* in its double sense as both noun (*gold*) and conjunction (*now*), thereby referring reflexively to the cycle of "Grands Faits Divers" themselves since the "now," by "stopping time momentarily," signals "what a *fait-divers* does, a 'flash' (newsbrief)," as in what the text itself will name as the "instant venu ostentatoire" ("come the showy moment [of a financial crash]").[47]

It is nonetheless the case that Mallarmé is hardly celebrating journalism here. As one would expect, he castigates its language—"the universal journalistic style"[48]—which he compares to money—"vain universal divinity" (335)—in that both strive for an unmediated relation between representation and object: "direct and palpable." Further, the result of that language is a dreary grayness that Mallarmé compares to the page of the newspaper itself, that flat "journal éployé" ("spread-open newspaper" 386), which depends on the aggressiveness of its headlines, its typographic variations, to produce the ersatz of feeling. Whereas poetry contains its own music, and this "par le privilège d'offrir, sans cet artifice de typographie, le repos vocal qui mesure l'élan" ("through the privilege of offering, without that artifice of typography, the vocal repose [through measured lines] that measures the élan [of one breath or one line]" 368).

Indeed, music is one of the sources of experience that Mallarmé repeatedly characterizes as golden ("an orchestra only marking with its gold").[49] To this can be added sunsets, moonrises ("this gold moonrise"), the book ("O golden clasps of old missals!"), light ("shafts of vibratory gold"), and, of course, the sun itself, which by extension, as a glittering star, becomes a version of the Mallarméan *lustre* that "scintillates in a thousand glances, now [*or*], like gold, an ambiguous smile. . . ."[50]

In this sense Mallarmé's poetic gold joins hands with Gide's counterfeit coin, since it was that coin's crystal center that, paradoxically, could represent the signifier's abstract purity. For, when stripped of its commodified exchange value, this coin was instead endowed by the modernist artist with the substitutional condition of the sign in its continual play of circulation.

It might be easy to read the lesson articulated by Goux's model as merely equating the abandonment of the gold standard with the rise of abstraction. With gold seen as equivalent to nature—epitomized by the sun—Malevich's *Victory over the Sun* (1913) would then stand as a declaration of the modernist position, its defiant antimaterialism, its refusal of any identifiable referent. But Goux's model is more complex than just marking an allegiance to abstraction understood as an idealist transcendence of material reality. The structuralist system through which markers of wealth as well as linguistic signs circulate may have cut off a direct connection to the referent, but the sign itself takes on a special kind of material presence.

Mallarmé celebrates this in the unexpected connection he makes between poetic language and money in the *fait-divers* called "Gold."

In "Gold," this comparison between the gold of the political economy and of the poet is established by the possible but unrealized comparison of a financial crash to a shipwreck. The extravagant display of huge amounts of wealth going up in flames would then be like a "phantasmagoric sunset" into which "a liquefaction of treasure creeps, flushing crimson and gold at the horizon." Unfortunately, however, "If a Bank fails [there is only] vagueness, mediocrity, grayness" (336). And this grayness seems to be in direct proportion to the precision with which the universal equivalent of money—"Cash (*le numéraire*), a device of terrible precision"—registers the catastrophe of failure, since it is this very precision, expressed in numbers, that leaves the reader of these reports totally cold. And Mallarmé focuses on the paradox that the more zeroes added to a figure, even as these push it farther and farther toward the "grandiloquence" of an astronomical sum, the more an effect of subtraction takes over as the number "loses any meaning" for our imaginations and begins to recede: "signifying that its totality equals almost nothing, spiritually."

But when he speaks of the "abstract shine" of the writer's gold, which money fails to possess, this abstraction itself needs to be given the particular cast of Mallarmé's *or*, which, as Cohn has reminded us, is also the conjunction "now," or "whereas." Thus, as a syncategoreme, a word that marks the here and now of its own position (either syntactic or physical, which is to say, either logical, temporal, or spatial), *or* has the possibility of operating against the grain of abstraction under-stood as a kind of idealist unity. This is the reading that Jacques Derrida stresses in order to disengage Mallarmé from the lit-erary-critical notion of an interplay of themes built on the slippage of polysemy. Going far beyond Cohn's interpretation of the "Or" of Mallarmé's title as only a temporal "now" that signifies *news flash*, Derrida argues that it is the very uncon-trollability of the physical spread of OR over the page of the text—"*dehORs*" ("outdoORs"), "*fantasmagORique*" "*trésOR*" ("stORe"), "*hORizon*," "*majORe*" ("mORe"), "*hORs*" ("ex-teriOR")—that makes OR a signifier truly cut free of the gold standard of even its most shifting signified.[51] For it is in this condition, to which Derrida gives the name "dissemination," that it can approach the "vacant sonority" of the music dreamed by Mallarmé in the poem "Igitur," where "*son or*" ("its gold") and "*sonore*" ("sonorous") play against one an-other in the relationship that Derrida calls "re-marking." By this he means folding over one another to produce both the replication of the series and difference of the same from itself. The character of the re-mark here is to produce a lateral pres-sure that "transforms the possessive adjective into a noun, *le* SON *or* ['the sound, "or"'], and the noun into an adjective *le son* OR ['the sound *or*']. The 'sound *or*' re-marks the signifier *or* (the phonic signifier : of the conjunction or of the noun, which latter is also the signifier of the substance or of the metallic signifier, etc.), but it also re-marks music."[52]

It is this folding over of the "re-mark" that, as it produces

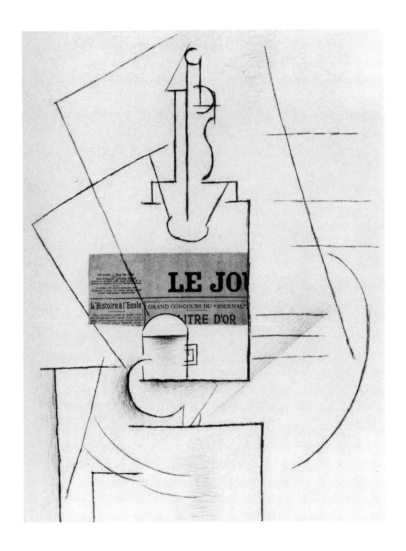

11.

Bottle, Cup and Newspaper

autumn–winter 1912

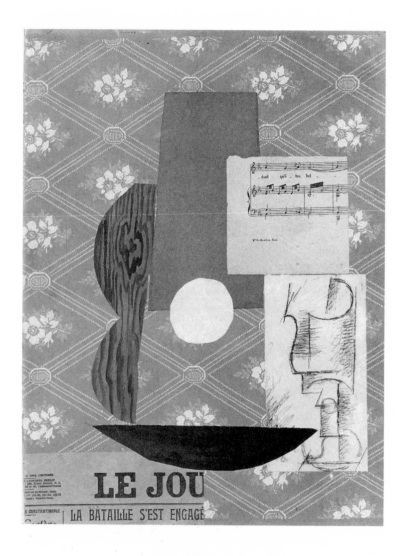

12.

Guitar, Sheet-music and Glass

autumn 1912

a syntactic and grammatic (not to mention semic) split into nonidentical pairs within one and the same signifier, makes one think of the structural play within Picasso's collage where the same operations of the fold and its "re-mark" yield the same aesthetic "gold." For there, as well, the collage pieces bifurcate, opening onto the "fiction" (Mallarmé's desire for language) of their signifieds—*shape* and *atmosphere* wrought from identical newspaper segments—as well as their utterances—the murmur of the aesthete doubling the speech of the shop girl.

One of the bifurcated utterances most historians of Picasso's collage seem to agree on is the one enunciated in what is perhaps the first of the series in the fall of 1912 (Fig. 12), where the newsprint says, "La bataille s'est engagée." This headline, which truncates the original announcement concerning the war in the Balkans ("La bataille s'est engagée furieuse sur les Lignes de Tchataldja" ["The battle is furiously joined at the Tchataldja front"]), also cuts the master title of the newspaper from LE JOURNAL to LE JOU. Given the "play" of the collage operation itself, scholars have tended to see the ensemble of words as working on two different levels, one addressing the Balkans, the other the aesthetic battle unleashed by collage either against the "high" of oil painting or against the (traditional) system of iconic representation still visible in the (now superseded) analytic cubist drawing of a glass juxtaposed to the other paper fragments.[53] One interpreter, however, triangulates this dialogical space, adding a voice that at this point could only be identified as Picasso's own.[54] For this speaker is seen as fighting a somewhat more personal "battle" than either that of political engagement with the left's resistance to interference in the Balkans or that of modernism's revaluation of artistic media. In this interpretation the speaker, understood as Picasso, is targeting the Section d'Or exhibition that opened in October to enthusiastic response from many avant-garde patrons and critics, among whom figured, most distressingly from Picasso's point of view, Apollinaire himself. Which means that in the fall of 1912 another, more partisan sense of "gold" is circulating within the collage sequence.

It was in the context of the Section d'Or show that Apollinaire gave his lecture "The Dismemberment of Cubism," in praise of a younger generation than that of Picasso and Braque, one to which Apollinaire was now consigning the future of the avant-garde.[55] The *or* of the Section d'Or was, of course, the Platonic notion of the Golden Section or an abstract system of proportion that was to open painting onto a unified, harmonic ideal. Delaunay, whose cubist variant Apollinaire baptised "Orphic" in reference to its musicality and its supposed abstraction, had made his house available to Apollinaire all through the fall; and the poet was to go on to write his conversation poem "Windows" as the catalog for Delaunay's January 1913 show in Munich.

But this excitement on Apollinaire's part over what Picasso undoubtedly considered a move to outflank him on his right—Orphism being stylistically more reactionary than cubism—was matched by Apollinaire's sudden enthusiasm for a challenge on cubism's cultural and political "left," in the form of futurism. Both Picasso and Apollinaire had visited the futurist exhibition in February 1912, and the poet, taking his cue from the painter's distaste, had written a critical review of the movement ("The Italian futurists declare that they will not abandon the advantages inherent in the subject, and it is precisely this that may prove to be the reef upon which all their artistic goodwill will be dashed to bits").[56] Over the succeeding months this was to change radically, however, as Apollinaire was swept up in the futurist call for breaking the barriers between art and life.

Perhaps the impetus was the sudden appearance on the Paris scene of Blaise Cendrars, who with his poem "Pâques à New York" was putting pressure on Apollinaire to distance himself from what could be seen as his outmoded allegiance to symbolism. Apollinaire's response was immediate. Changing the title of his forthcoming book of poems from *Eau de vie* (too symbolist) to *Alcools* (more populist, more sexy), he began running around Paris with Léger to look at the urban iconography of billboards and street signs, writing the manifesto for the futurist magazine *Lacerba* where he praises Marinetti's "Words in Freedom," and generally espousing what he called "l'esprit nouveau."[57]

Picasso, we know, disliked futurism. He hated the futurist philosophizing about art in the name of "advanced" ideas such as dynamism, subjectivism, and objectivism. "That kind of chatter gave Picasso the horrors," Severini reported, quoting him as complaining: "What's the point of yammering on like that?" Picasso is supposed to have interrupted a futurist discussion about the need for modern subjects, such as racing cars (more beautiful than the Nike of Samothrace) or armored trucks, by shouting: "One can make a modern subject out of Greek warriors."[58]

But apart from the many things that Picasso would have disliked about futurism—from its claims to have outdistanced him even though it clung to the naturalist referent (no matter how disguised); to the ultimately monologic space (despite the typographic noisiness) of its "Words in Freedom," so foreign to the bifurcating "re-mark" of his own use of words; to its colonization of Apollinaire, which, given the constrictedness of Picasso's "subculture," was a serious threat indeed—there was also futurism's intrusion into his private life in the form of Fernande's new relationship to Ubaldo Oppi. In a letter to Braque in May of 1912 Picasso gives the flavor of his personal disgust: "Fernande has left with a Futurist. What am I going to do with the dog?" And throughout the summer Fernande continued to plague him. She not only made the complicated move of his studio from Montmartre to Montparnasse even more unpleasant [59] but went to Céret, where Picasso had intended to summer with his new companion, Marcelle Humbert (whom he renamed Eva Gouel). Picasso testifies to his worry about becoming a potential *fait-divers* himself: "I'm really annoyed by all this because I don't want my love for Marcelle to be hurt in any way by any trouble they [the newspapers] could make for me," he writes to Braque in June.[60]

From the subject who speaks, to the object who is journalistically "spoken," Picasso joins the conversation that circulates in the polyphonic space of the collages. But his is only one voice, itself bifurcated. Many other voices attach to these speakers, all of them doubling and tripling from within. A small amount of text will do it. If the *fait-divers* depends on just enough "reality" for the circulation of rumor, the collages have just enough meaning for the circulation of the sign, while the signifiers are in vivid enough circulation to trigger the constellation of the signified, as it moves between Mallarmé's "fiction" and Gide's "counterfeit."

Picasso / Pastiche

I passed my own brand of anxiety along to you and you assimilated it.

—Picasso to Françoise Gilot

HISTORIANS ARE IMPRESSED BY THIS SCENE: A gray April day in 1916, the big echoing studio on the rue Schoelcher with its wild disorder but from which something—the frail young woman—is now missing; the hundreds and hundreds of canvases piled on tables and easels and stacked against the wall like the scales of so many giant fish but from which something—the terrifying black and red Harlequin with his sinister white grimace (Fig. 13)—is also now missing.[1]

Yet it had been there on that earlier day, back in December of 1915, riding one of the large central easels, drawing to itself all the cold glitter raining in from the high banks of windows, and attracting Jean Cocteau's excited attention.[2] A death sentinel, the picture had been what Picasso had pointed to as he told them that his companion, Eva, was dying. But underneath the solemnity the young Cocteau had perceived an edgy excitement in the older man's voice; and even though it was to Gertrude Stein and not to him that Picasso had confessed his belief that the picture "is the best that I have done,"³ Cocteau could see past the heaps of paper and bric-à-brac littering the floor, with the strange eruption here and there of an African sculpture, and the steady crunch of discarded tubes of paint as one walked—could see past this chaos to the order that had been mortised into this image to give it its harsh authority.⁴

On that winter day when Satie had brought him to see Picasso, this was an authority Cocteau did not yet understand. But, what was far more important, he could see Picasso's identification with it. And for Cocteau, who had come on a secret mission, it was what fate had handed over to him, the key to the master. Which is why the following April, in preparation for this scene art historians find so impressive, he had gone to one of the theater rental shops behind the Opéra to procure a Harlequin costume for his long-contemplated return to the rue Schoelcher. And he had not been wrong. As he took off his trench coat to expose his tight satin tunic with its motley of diamonds—yellow, blue, and pink—all etched with sequins, he could see the mischievous wreath of Picasso's grin, accepting his gift.⁵

If they are impressed by this scene, now, it is because it not only seems to encapsulate the drama of the sudden change that was to occur in Picasso's work but also appears to explain it. On the one hand, they say, there was the loneliness and the sadness, a deadened wartime Paris, emptied of all his clos-

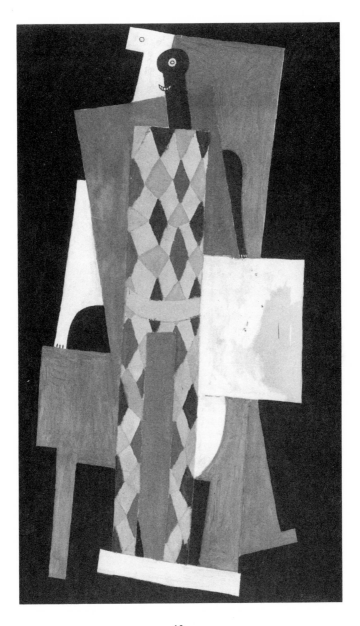

13.
Harlequin
autumn 1915

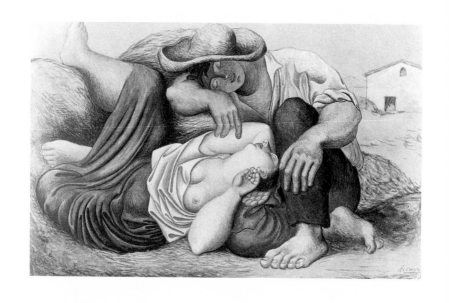

14.
Sleeping Peasants
1919

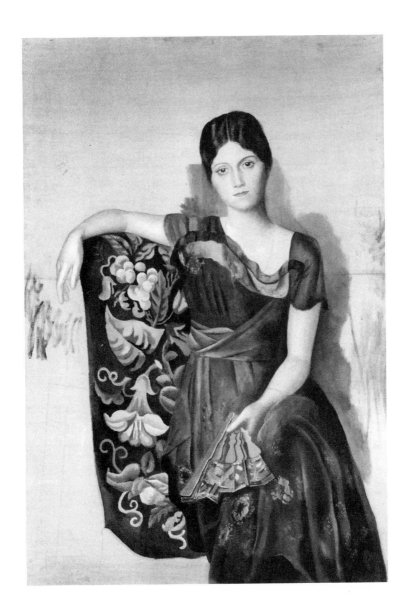

15.
Olga Picasso in an Armchair
autumn 1917

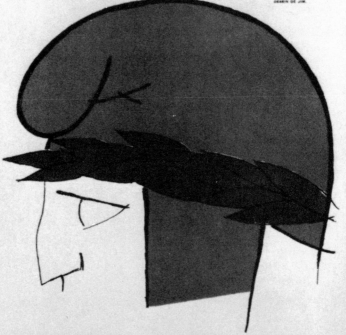

16.

Jean Cocteau, *Dante avec nous*

June 15, 1915

est companions, yet a Paris strangely alive with a new hostility as angry strangers in this post-Verdun uncertainty thrust white feathers at him on the streets. On the other hand, the commentators note, there was the diversion Cocteau offered along with the shameless flattery, and the alluring possibility of escape. By 1916 Picasso had begun to feel himself in chains, the story runs, surrounded by a lot of dour believers for whom the only acceptable altar for their cult was a café table laid with the requisite objects, the glass, the lemon, the newspaper, the tobacco pouch, the guitar. Viewing the situation now, through the eyes of this sophisticated youngster, this emissary from the world of international ballet, he began to see the narrow provincialism of it all, the folkloristic cant of what had, only two years before, seemed disruptive and daring.

So the commentators have no trouble whatever crediting Cocteau with what he claims, his position as the Pied Piper of Picasso's march toward Rome for his embrace of the musical theater with all its ornament and spectacle and with all its scenographically realist demands: "I led him to that," Cocteau says. "His entourage couldn't believe he would follow me. A dictatorship weighed on Montmartre and Montparnasse. They were passing through the austere phase of cubism. The objects that could stand on a café table, the Spanish guitar, these were the only pleasures allowed. To paint a decor, above all at the Ballet Russe . . . was a crime."[6]

The momentousness of this turning in Picasso's work can be grasped in part from the negative reception of the results that began to surface by the end of the teens. Picasso had labored long and hard for the show he mounted in 1919 for his new dealer, Paul Rosenberg, the first one-man show he had had in thirteen years. But Roger Allard's review dismissed it as nothing but historical pastiche: "Everything, including Leonardo, Dürer, Le Nain, Ingres, Van Gogh, Cézanne, yes, everything. . . . except Picasso," he lamented.[7]

It is the accusation of pastiche that signals the momentousness of this critique, for in many eyes it opens cubism itself to question: cubism, the one thing that Picasso—seemingly so impervious to the opinions of others—would always jealously guard as *his*. Years later, when he was accused at a Communist Congress in Poland of being an impressionist-surrealist, he was to turn on the Party hack with the haughty rejoinder that "if he wanted to insult me at least he should get his terminology straight and damn me for being the inventor of Cubism."[8] But it is precisely cubism that falls victim to the invective of pastiche if we accept a point of view such as Delaunay took in 1923 and see Picasso's cubism itself as nothing more than a clever imitation of Braque. "Picasso with his periods," Delaunay was to sneer, "Steinlen, Lautrec, Van Gogh, Daumier, Corot, negroes, Braque, Derain, Cézanne, Renoir, Ingres, etc. etc. etc. Puvis de Chavannes, neo-Italian . . . these influences prove the lack of seriousness, in terms of construction and sureness."[9]

Sixty years later, the same conclusion would be drawn, if less disdainfully, as Gérard Genette also named pastiche the matrix within which absolutely all of Picasso's work unfolded: "Picasso is only himself *through the vehicle of* the styles that belong successively to Lautrec, Braque, Ingres, etc., and Stravinsky by means of his access to impressionism, polytonality, neo-classicism and his late conversion to serial discipline."[10] This, we could say, is the immanent, though prejudicial, understanding of Picasso's relation to pastiche, for, depriving him of cubism, it leaves him no ground to stand on that could seriously be said to be *his*.

There is another interpretation of the phenomenon that also sees it as internal to Picasso's process but is entirely uncritical and invokes it without prejudice. Picasso, this argument goes, is not a *pasticheur*. He is merely following out the logic inherent within cubism itself once the incorporative principle of collage has been established. If one can glue a calling card or a postage stamp or a swatch of wallpaper onto a drawing, what is to prevent the conceptual enlargement of this procedure to encompass the world of Old Master imagery, as well as the imitation of the wide variety of mediums—from sculpture to tapestry, from stained glass to engraved gems—in which this museum culture comes? Proponents of this interpretation call this not pastiche but rather the "access" that Picasso had patiently and legitimately gained to the *musée imaginaire*.

The endogenous description of the phenomenon can thus range in its final assessment from Delaunay's horrified dismissal of Picasso's "continuity in pillage" to the art historian's pleasure at Picasso's force of synthesis, whether in combining Le Nain and Ingres to form a new sense of Frenchness[11] or in fusing archaic sculpture, Raphael, and photography to assert the continuity of painting-as-such within the museum without walls.[12]

In contradistinction to the internal form of the explanation, there is, of course, the externalist one. This type we have already witnessed in action, and we have heard its accents in the guise of Cocteau's declaration "It was I who led him." Like the internal analyses, externalist explanations are also multiple, moving from Picasso's private life, to his social mobility, to the political situation in which he suddenly found himself with the outbreak of war. Thus it was not the bourgeoisification but the politics of the thing that William Uhde stuck at as he, too, stared at the 1919 exhibition, stupefied:

> I found myself in the presence of a huge portrait in what is known as the Ingres manner; the conventionality, the sobriety of the attitude seemed studied, and it seemed to be repressing some pathetic secret. . . . What was the meaning of this and the other pictures I saw on that occasion? Were they but an interlude, a gesture—splendid but without significance—which the hand made, while the soul, worn out on its long journey, rested? Or was it that at this time when men were ruled by hate, when Roman circumspection, conscious of itself, stood out against the cloudy metaphysical German habits of thought, he felt that innumerable people were pointing their fingers at him, reproaching him with having strong German sympathies and accusing him of being secretly in connivance with the enemy? . . . Was he trying def-

initely to range himself on the French side, and did these pictures attest to the torment of his soul?[13]

Uhde is telegraphing here what would be developed at far greater length and in far greater detail in recent accounts of the outbursts of French nationalism during World War I, which in turn prepared the way for the postwar *rappel à l'ordre*. Cubism, having been labeled "boche" as early as 1914, its very spelling having been retailored along German lines—as the *c* of cube was steadily changed to a *k* under the pen of a hostile press—a whole host of different styles with greater claims to "Frenchness" were now being adopted, ranging from *images d'Epinal* to a classicized revision of art nouveau. And the practitioners of these styles came from the ranks of the former cubists or fringe cubists themselves as well as from younger, opportunistic fellow travelers in the art world, such as Ozenfant, and Cocteau (Fig. 16). Picasso's desertion of cubism thus aligns with something in the air, this argument runs, and is barely in need of further, more case-specific elaboration.[14]

These are the ones, thus, for whom the scene at the rue Schoelcher, with Cocteau in his Harlequin outfit, carries a certain explanatory force in relation to Picasso's conversion, although for them it was politics, not death, that had softened him up, preparing him for the pluralism of Cocteau's brand of patriotism, his "anything goes, as long as it's French."

But we still have to imagine it . . . to grasp the immensity of the confidence game that Cocteau is supposed to have pulled off, if indeed we are to credit the arrogance of his boast "It was I who led him." That is, we have to remember that Cocteau was basically "Jeanchik," the very young man who as a precocious high school graduate had written a totally symbolist ballet for the Ballet Russe, in turn provoking Diaghilev to deliver to this late adolescent one of the great lessons in the logic of the twentieth-century culture of the spectacle. Shrugging off what had been the retrograde elegance of Cocteau's first contribution, Diaghilev had instead commanded: "Astonish me!" And like the art directors of so many Madison Avenue advertising firms a half century later, Cocteau was to realize that the fields in which to prospect for the shock necessary to this effect were not those of Elysium but the *terrains vagues* of the shabby studios of the avant-garde.

Fresh from the offices of *Le Mot*, the patriotic review ("the *métèque* ["half-breed"] cannot love our journal") with pretensions to becoming the arbiter of an emerging cultural chic ("the tact of understanding just how far you can go too far"), and so involved in trafficking in the stereotype of the bohemian artist that he felt obliged to adopt the tones of a slumming dandy in order to describe Picasso's reaction to the figure he, Cocteau, had cut during an August afternoon they spent together—"gloves, cane and collar astonish these artists in shirtsleeves" (this despite the fact that Picasso and his friends all happened to be wearing jackets and ties)—Cocteau was desperate in 1916 to grab and hold Picasso's attention.[15] He needed this trophy to bring to Diaghilev, to make up for the humiliating rebuff he had suffered when Stravinsky had earlier refused to work with him. He had brought his mother's camera to the lunch he was to have with Picasso and his band and he had spent hours ingratiating himself with them, photographing their antics, only to write the next day to a friend: "Nothing very new except that Picasso takes me to the Rotonde. I never stay more than a moment, despite the flattering welcome." Cocteau had waited those four months for his moment, from the day in April 1916 at the rue Schoelcher to this mid-August afternoon. He was working on a ballet with Satie, whom he had convinced to do the music the year before. Now he wanted Picasso for the sets. But he had still said nothing about his idea on that day in May when he had sat for a portrait drawing for Picasso—"an Ingres head of me," he called it (Fig. 31).[16]

Which brings us to the dubiousness with which Pierre Daix views the whole Cocteau narrative and the idea that Picasso should have had the need of *any* leash to lead him into his postcubist classicism, particularly a leash as frail as Cocteau's.[17] The first of Picasso's Ingresque portraits, the one of Max Jacob (Fig. 29), was made in January 1915, Daix points out, and the second, of Vollard (Fig. 30), in August of the same year—ten months before Cocteau's was even thought of. For Daix, the conditions for Picasso's classicism had already been put in place as early as 1913, the minute Picasso's cardboard constructions began to allow the cubist syntax to test, and be tested by, the parameters of real space. After this, in early 1914, fragments of perspective play a flirtatious game with flattened geometric profiles of cut paper, such that Renaissance space nests inside the overarching cubist proposition the way that, say, Newtonian physics exists as a special case of the general theory of relativity (see Fig. 53).[18]

Thus Daix mounts the most endogenous argument of them all, in which Picasso, having taken up portraiture in an Ingresque manner, "didn't leave cubism" at all. "We never see him compromise his fundamental discoveries of the cubist period," Daix says of the post–Ballet Russe, post-Olga Picasso. "There is no falling off, no break, even if his cubism becomes classical, which is to say not primitive but perfect."[19]

This brings Daix almost but not quite into line with what Picasso told Ernst Ansermet in Rome. It was spring 1917 and Picasso, working on the *Parade* sets, had taken a studio facing the Villa Medici. There he practiced an alternation between naturalist scenes and cubist drawings. Ansermet found this stylistic schizophrenia peculiar and he wondered about it to Picasso. "But can't you see?" Picasso said. "The results are the same."[20]

Daix wants the Ingresque portraits to remain cubist, their pockets of modeling dispersed over the laconic whiteness of the page, with its fairly noncommittal allusions to a third dimension, like so many quotations of a classical style they both master and hold at arm's length. But Picasso, installed in Rome, has gone much farther than the Max Jacob or Vollard portraits, permitting himself undiluted copies of Ingres (Fig. 18) that would eventuate in paintings such as the *Olga Picasso in an Armchair* (Fig. 15), as well as copies of Corot (Fig. 37), and of postcard snapshots of peasant girls (Fig. 19), all involv-

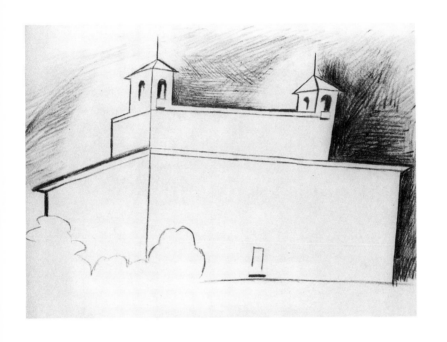

17.
Villa Medici
1917

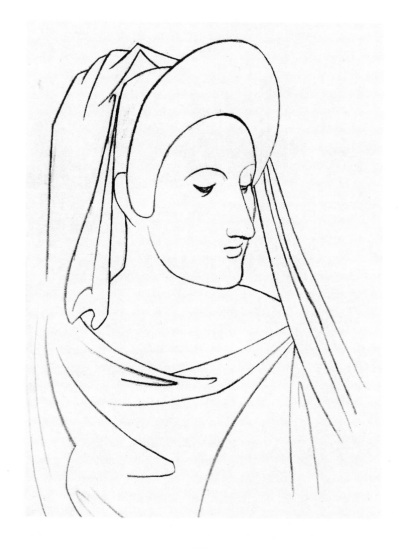

18.
After Ingres's Tu Marcellus Eris
1917

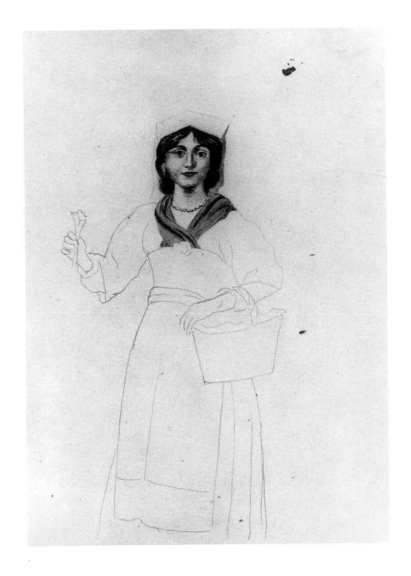

19.
Italian Flower Girl
1917

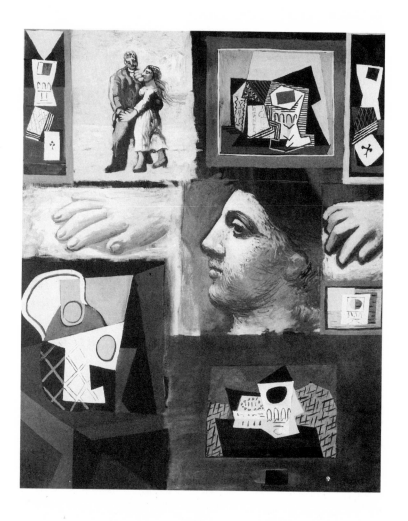

20.
Studies
1920

ing a spatial realism in which nothing is in cubist brackets, nothing in the second degree. If Daix says even here, "Can't you see, the results are the same," it's because Picasso has already produced the formula. But this only begs the question of how Picasso could ever have said it and meant it.

This is Picasso after all, the artist who faulted even analytic cubism for being "basically in perspective,"[21] the artist who from the early days of the Bateau-Lavoir had identified all versions of nineteenth-century classicism, even Degas's, as his enemy. The *bande à Picasso* used to practice perfecting their collective disdain in the game they called "Playing Degas." André Salmon recalls: "One of us does Degas, famous grumbler, visiting Pablo and 'judging' him. But it doesn't have to be Degas—it could very well be Puvis de Chavanne, or Bonnet, or Bouguerreau, or Courbet, or even Baudelaire working up a *Salon*. Picasso would laugh at the barbs thrown at him, for, I want to insist, no one was sparing in those fine days."[22] After all that, how was it possible, only ten years later and with only three years separating him from some of his greatest cubist inventions, for Picasso to stick a top hat on his head, gaze at himself in the mirror, and murmur, "Monsieur Ingres" before the wide-eyed Ansermet?[23] An Ingres who leaps back and forth between cubism and a pastiche of many other styles, including classicism, because "the results are the same"?

The externalist arguments about the change in Picasso's style in 1916–17 and the onset of pastiche can afford to condescend to the results: after all, this is a Picasso aping his inferiors. The endogenous arguments can only praise what in various ways they term his powers of synthesis, since whatever wells up from the master must be a result of his perfect control. But what if we read the "Can't you see the results are the same" symptomatically? Which is to say, the declaration in good faith of something that is false on its face. Then we could state what seems far more justifiably the fact: that between 1916 and 1924, as pastiche became more and more the medium in which he practiced, Picasso did increasingly fatuous work—arch, decorative, empty—work that seems unreconcilable with the formal rigor of cubism and yet, given the unrivaled example of that earlier brilliance, work that must somehow issue from a logic internal to it and not from a set of external circumstances. The logic of the symptom would, then, be endogenous and prejudicial, but it would not claim cubism as the happy accident of Picasso imitating Braque. Rather, it would seek the etiology of pastiche, the internal conditions for its onset. Considering pastiche symptomatically—as an aesthetic breakdown, as it were—it would fashion its project of historical explanation along something like a medical model. But not an epidemiology; a psychopathology rather—something like the psychopathology of the artist's practical life.

· · ·

A young American journalist with a prodigious knowledge of modern art went to interview Kahnweiler. It was the mid-1960s, a short time after Françoise Gilot's *Life with Picasso* had made its appearance, to the rage of the master and the dismay of his friends. Liking the young woman, Kahnweiler asked her to read the book and tell him frankly what she thought. "The American perspective," he said, seeming already to have anticipated her entirely unshocked reaction. As she acknowledged her pleasure in the book and how much she had learned, she saw she was paining him.[24] But he could not tell her how and in what way he found this account so wholly offensive.

The easiest and most obvious thing, of course, is Gilot's nastiness on the subject of the then-reigning queen, Jacqueline Roque Picasso, who is made out in the book's final pages to be an opportunistic also-ran, a caretaker whom Picasso merely accepted in the end, the ultimate doormat. But perhaps there is a "dirty secret" in *Life with Picasso* that is not as peripheral to the master as the conditions of his acquiring Jacqueline. Perhaps there is the continuous and vivid dramatization of what the book terms Picasso's "constant dread of death," to which Picasso himself refers in the end when he threatens Gilot: "You made your life with me, I passed my own brand of anxiety along to you and you assimilated it."[25] If attaching the word *anxiety* to Picasso's name is almost unthinkable, so assured and effortless was his production, so secure a grip did he seem to have on the reins of his life, it is nonetheless the case that anxiety is what is amply demonstrated in the course of these pages.[26] It is there in the daily ritual of Picasso's awakening, during which he is slowly and laboriously coaxed out of each morning's despair, with its lamentation about his health, his friends, his work, and its compulsion to keep scratching the scab that comes in the form of Olga's daily letter of abuse.[27] It is there in what Gilot calls "the disease of the will that made it impossible for him to make the slightest domestic decision," a disease that produces the frequent scenes during which Picasso argues with an irrational persistence about whether to go on a trip or to a bullfight and eventually reduces his interlocutors to tears.[28] Or it is there in his fanatical superstitiousness, ranging from the taboo against hats on beds or bread placed badly on the table, to the ritual of silence imposed on everyone before leaving on a trip, to the fear of having his hair cut lest his bodily substances fall into hostile hands.[29] For most of the readers of *Life with Picasso* such details seem merely picturesque, the personal eccentricities freely granted to the man of genius. But for Kahnweiler, as well as his other friends, perhaps it was the very fact that this was a Picasso they recognized but could not square with the antic side of his personality that gave these revelations the obscene quality of the vulgar indiscretion.

That anxiety should have been Picasso's daily companion is, however, interesting to the analysis I wish to mount here. This is not because I want to probe his private life—indeed, my analysis has nothing to do with it. Rather, the psychoanalytic model of anxiety puts in place a particular structure, called reaction formation. And I will be maintaining that reaction formation, itself a transformational system, is particularly apposite in this case. For this is a dialectical structure in which prohibited desires are turned into their opposite—anal eroticism converted, for example, into obsessional cleanliness or conscientiousness—to form the means of warding off the danger that could come from the prohibition *and* the possibility of continuing to transgress covertly; Freud gives as an example of reaction formation the compulsive hand washer whose conduct not only defends against masturbatory desire, providing as a "secondary gain" the display of the subject's drive for purity, but becomes a way *as well* of enacting and thereby gratifying the very behavior that has been repressed.*

---

*The two important parts of Freud's model come from the overall nature of anxiety on the one hand—that it is a reaction to a signal of danger—and, on the other, from the nature of reaction formation itself as characteristic of the symptomatic behavior of the anxious subject—most often analyzed by Freud in the guise of obsessional neurosis. In both these aspects we encounter the dialectical character of the phenomenon. Produced by the ego, anxiety is a function of the reality principle as the ego defends itself against external threat. Yet since threat itself is often perceived by the subject as a response to something he has himself initiated, that is, to instinctual desires arising from within, the defense against such danger can be to eliminate the threat by repressing the desires or, through other processes of symptom formation, by changing the outward manifestation of those desires. Thus the ego defends itself against anxiety by the creation of the symptom. Yet the symptom, Freud continues, turns out to be a defense that is its own form of threat, because as the ego incorporates the symptom into its own manner of processing reality, it finds itself in the position of having smuggled the enemy within its gates. The symptom, Freud writes, "being the true substitute for and derivative of the repressed impulse, carries on the role of the latter; it continually renews its demands for satisfaction and thus obliges the ego in its turn to give the signal of unpleasure and put itself in a posture of defense" (*Inhibitions, Symptoms and Anxiety*, trans. Alix Strachey [New York: Norton, 1959], 21).

If the inside/outside oscillation in the source of anxiety is one aspect of its dialectical condition, the other is in the structure of the symptoms themselves in either their negative form as prohibitions, precautions, and expiations or in their positive guise as substitutive satisfactions. For insofar as the symptoms are merely inverted versions of the instincts they are supposed to defend against, they not only allow a distorted form of the instinctual drive to continue to

And, I would argue, it is precisely in this structure of duplicity that this model for systematic conversion can form an explanatory paradigm for Picasso's operation of pastiche.

• • •

It's 1917 in Montrouge, the suburb just south of Paris to which Picasso has moved the previous October. Picasso has just fashioned a self-portrait (Fig. 22) that in Sabartès's estimation is "the least characteristic" of any he will ever do: "It's as though he made it just to be doing something; as though he took it into his head to draw himself so as not to think of other things or, so to say, without conviction."[30] The implication is that the work comes from the last two months of the year, after Picasso's return from Spain with Olga, a premonition of the emotional roller coaster that lay ahead. But it could also date from the opening months, just before the departure in late February for Rome and the long interlude of working on *Parade*.

---

seek out satisfaction but, through the logic of a secondary gain, also provide the ego with narcissistic gratification from the very form the symptom has taken, as in the case of the obsessional neurotic who feels better, because cleaner or more conscientious, than others. Thus even as they work to deeroticize the instincts, thereby allowing them to enter the realm of the ego no longer in the form of pleasure but in the guise, now, of compulsion, the symptoms simultaneously have just the opposite effect as they operate secretly to reeroticize whole realms of reality testing by setting up the compulsive behavior itself as a covert form of the prohibited impulse, which is thereby allowed to approach ever more closely to satisfaction. "The symptom-formation scores a triumph," Freud writes of this aspect, "if it succeeds in combining the prohibition with satisfaction so that what was originally a defensive command or prohibition acquires the significance of a satisfaction as well" (Ibid., 37).

The striking thing about the drawing is its brute juxtaposition of aggressively modeled head with extremely cursive body: the barest outlines of a suited torso seated in a chair and shown in three-quarters profile. None of Picasso's other classical portraits push this far toward a burlesque of Ingres's tendency to polarize his drawings between the modeled and the flat; all of the early ones (Jacob, Vollard) distribute the modeling of the face outward into the hands and parts of the clothing as well, while the later ones (Apollinaire, Rosenberg, Stravinsky [Fig. 32], Madame Wildenstein) largely suppress the modeling altogether.

There is, however, an intermediary object that could explain the particularly strident form of Picasso's "Ingrism" here, as well as what Sabartès takes to be the disheartened mood of the sitter. That object is another portrait (Fig. 23), published in the January 1917 issue of *391* and intended to parody Picasso's new stylistic departure as that had been made widely available to the art world through the reproduction of the Jacob and Vollard portraits in the December issue of *Elan* just one month before. Accompanied by the mocking notice "Picasso Repentant," the work, which is by Picabia, shows the critic Max Goth in three-quarters profile in a chair, everything but his head delivered in crudely simplified outline, the head itself, however, presented in high relief by means of a pasted-on photograph. Sneering that Picasso has fled cubism "to return to the Ecole des Beaux-Arts" and paint from the model, the commentary notes that "Picasso is henceforth the head of a new school to which our collaborator Francis Picabia has not hesitated for a moment to pledge allegiance. The Kodak published above is its solemn token." And indeed, with the comparison between the Picasso and the Picabia in place, it does strike one that the mode of address in Picasso's rendition of his own head is based less on the formal quality of Ingres's draftsmanship than on the tonal distributions characteristic of a photograph.

The hypothesis I would like to entertain, based on this comparison, is that Picasso noticed Picabia's pastiche of his new stylistic departure, noticed it and confirmed it with his own version of the same pastiche, producing thereby a strange derivative of a derivative, in the form of a pastiche of himself. I would further suggest that the part of Picabia's satire that Picasso would have found the least amusing, accounting thereby for the mood of his own image, would have been the insinuation of the photograph in what should have been the drawing's pride of place.

That Picasso had very little use for photography except as a way of documenting his own work has long been an assumption of Picasso scholarship. Cubism was, after all, the painstaking and thoroughgoing dismantling of unified, perspectival space, the very space that the camera, with its particular optics, could not but reproduce again and again. Brassaï seems to capture Picasso's attitude in the 1930s when he records Picasso, on discovering that the photographer had once been a gifted draftsman, exclaiming: "Why don't you go on with it? You own a gold mine, and you're exploiting a salt mine."[31] Fernande Olivier seems to second this with an an-

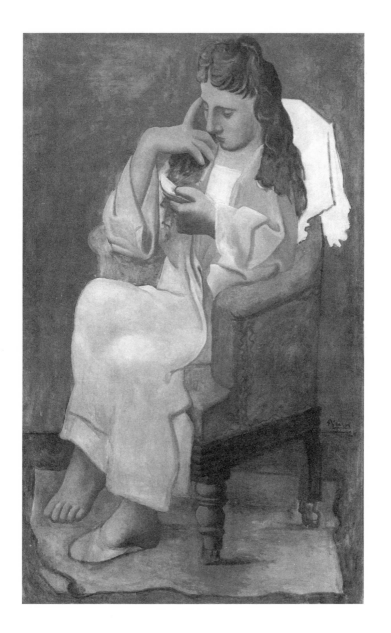

21.
Woman Reading
1920

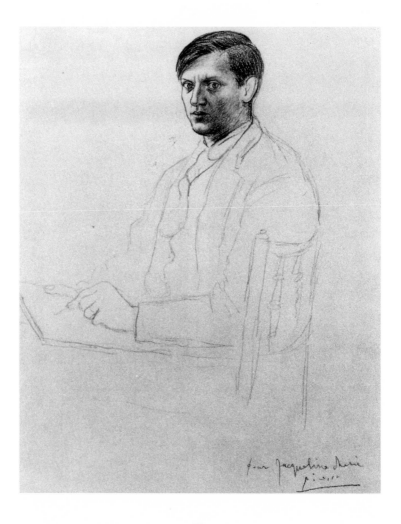

22.
Self–Portrait
1917

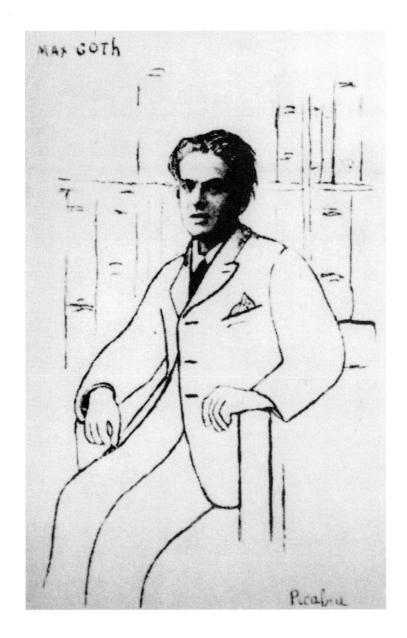

23.
Picabia, *Portrait of Max Goth*
1917

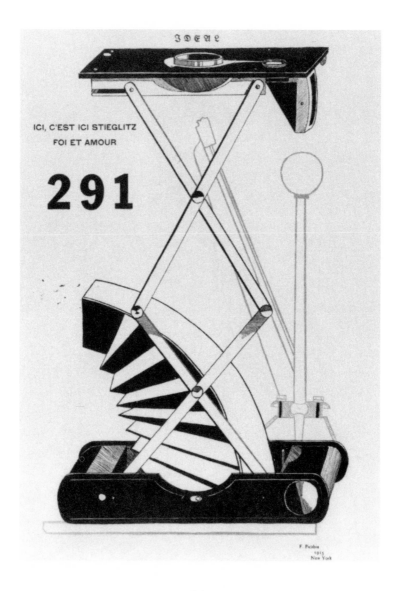

24.
Picabia, *Ici, C'est Ici Stieglitz*
1915

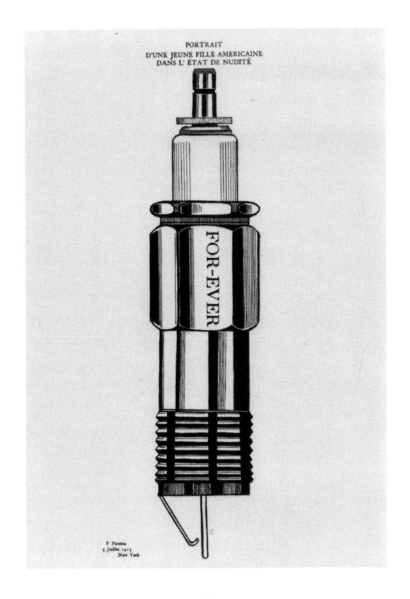

25.

Picabia, *Portrait d'une jeune fille americaine*

1915

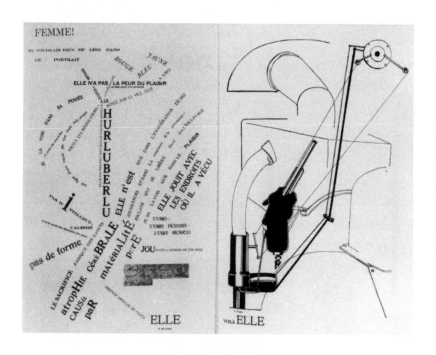

26.
Picabia, *Voilà* ELLE
1915

ecdote that comes from the opening days of cubist collage, in which an explorer tells Picasso about showing a photograph of himself to a tribal sculptor who fails to understand it as an image. Upon being told that it represents the explorer himself, the African contradicts him by making a drawing of his true "likeness" in the style of a fetish object, being careful to note the details of the European's uniform by wreathing his head with gold braid and the outline of his body with buttons.[32]

Very recent scholarship, however, is trying to discover a hitherto unknown "photographic project" on Picasso's part: to demonstrate the role that photography is supposed to have played in some of his most daring cubist insights, such as the extreme spatial ambiguities at Horta in 1909, or to assert that the very idea of collage is indebted to the photograph's automatic powers of synthesis, its "means of establishing relations from work to work, of allowing the play of associations, of contrasts, of possible new transformations," such that it was the photographs Picasso took of installations of his latest work on the studio wall that set up a "round-trip by means of the chemistry of film: from the drawing to the cliché, from the paper print to the pasted papers."[33]

This claim is based on what seems to me a wildly projective overinterpretation of the photographs Picasso made as documents, plus what would seem the patently absurd remark by Gertrude Stein in 1938 that the few photographs Picasso took of still-life arrangements in 1911 were so successful a visual transformation "that it wasn't even necessary for him to paint the painting";[34] it also suborns one of Fernande Olivier's anecdotes to make its point. Accordingly Anne Baldissari's *Picasso, Photographer* begins: " 'I've discovered photography. I could kill myself. I have nothing more to learn,' Pablo Picasso cried out, in the paroxysm of 'a nervous attack' provoked by taking hashish." Asserting that these "surprising words should be taken *literally* in reference to the specificity of his photographic experience," the writer wants to claim that Picasso's " 'discovery of photography' meant without any doubt that he considered himself to have appropriated its formal resources . . . [to have] discovered that it was capable, to the same extent as painting, of being a work. Discovered that in the exchanges between the two mediums nothing was yet decided, nothing yet forbidden."[35]

But to read Olivier's account in this way is to distort its implications wildly. For in the context of describing Picasso's move from the poverty of the Bateau-Lavoir to the relative luxury of the boulevard de Clichy, Fernande is telling about the regret that successful painters come to feel about leaving behind the site of their youthful enthusiasm and their most productively ardent struggles. She wants to describe Picasso's own passion for constant development, for the ceaseless formal research that will lead to change. The anecdote she chooses to illustrate this determination, by means of negative example, is the drug-provoked anxiety attack about "having nothing new to learn," which she goes on to elaborate as the photography-based "revelation that one day he would be frozen in his development. He would get to the end, a wall; he wouldn't be able to go any farther: he would have nothing more to learn, to discover, to know, to penetrate little by little all the secrets of an art that he wanted as if new."[36]

Far from being an ebullient "discovery" of the creative possibilities of photography, this would seem a nightmarish disclosure of the not-so-distant possibility of the automation of art, with an accompanying collapse of the patient analysis of vision and its careful construction of a pictorial analogue into its hideous opposite, namely, the image as "readymade." The language of frozen motion, of the wall, of nothing new to learn because everything is instantaneously exposed—all of this speaks of a phobic reaction against a mechanization of vision.

And in the early teens, photography was, indeed, being heralded as the newly objectivized way of producing art, an art appropriate to the "age of the machine." A typical example of this argument was published in both French and English in the September–October 1915 issue of *291*, in which Marius de Zayas lauds Stieglitz's *The Steerage* as the outcome of modern plastic expression's desire "to create for itself an objectivity," and Paul Haviland speaks of photography as the means to this objectivity, being the fruit of the union of man and the machine; "the camera," he adds, "is the image of [man's] eye; the machine is his 'daughter born without a mother.' "[37]

With the last citation, Haviland is, of course, acknowledging not only the full-page publication of Picabia's mechanomorphic drawing *Fille née sans mère* in the June issue of *291* but, even further, the decisive impact of Picabia on all the thinking of *291* and particularly that of Stieglitz and Zayas. Having begun during Picabia's first stay in New York in 1913, that fascination accelerated in the summer of 1915 after Picabia's second arrival. It is dramatized in the July-August issue, where, in the course of the usual celebration of the man/machine/photography equation, Zayas continues (in French and English): "Of all those who have come to conquer America, Picabia is the only one to have done it like Cortez. . . . The results have arrived. He has brought them to '291' which accepts them as an experiment, and publishes them with the conviction that they have the real value that all attempts at the discovery of an objective truth possess." And on the succeeding pages there follows the group of portraits by Picabia, in which Stieglitz, Haviland, Zayas, Picabia himself, and "an American girl in a state of nudity" are all represented as industrial objects or machine parts, their graphic presentation rendered through the icily impersonal crispness of mechanical drawing (Figs. 24, 25, 43, and 50).

It is known that this issue of *291* was available in Paris in late August of 1915, probably owing to the collaboration between Stieglitz's magazine and Apollinaire's *Les Soirées de Paris*, which Zayas had set up in spring of the year before.[38] Picasso, who returned to Paris in August for Eva to enter the hospital, began his portrait of Vollard the same month. And it is in Vollard's portrait, I would say, that the operations of reaction formation begin to be felt, as the pastiche of Ingres performs a reversal that is nonetheless a repetition of all the despised fruits of mechanomorphism: its frontality, its symmetry, its relentless linearity, its coldness, its (to say the word) classicism.

Picabia, it must be recalled, had been annoyingly in Picasso's sights for some time, ever since Apollinaire's enthusiasm over the two enormous abstract pictures Picabia showed at the Salon d'Automne in 1913.[39] In 1913, of course, the form that Picabia's idea of "objectivity" had taken was that of abstraction, voiced not only in the catalog preface to his one-man show at 291 but also in his urging Stieglitz to publish Kandinsky's *Concerning the Spiritual in Art* that same year in *Camera Work*. And Picasso's opposition to abstract art had always been adamant and unambiguous. Daix recalls that "Picasso would object vociferously if anyone told him that one of his paintings was abstract. . . . Picasso said to me of one work, 'That's a head.'—'That thing with the triangle,' I asked.—'But it's a head, it's a head.' In it there are a few small signs, like the eyes, that make the things spill over into a non-abstract universe."[40] If in 1910 and 1911 Picasso and Braque clung to small identifying details—like the drawer pull or the trompe l'oeil nail—Daix says, this was because they refused the abstraction that would otherwise gather around the simplified crystalline planes. "One must ask oneself," Daix continues, "why Picasso and Braque conceived and elaborated a system of representation that broke with illusionism, with perspective, only to produce a representation of reality that would function in the same manner: that the public was supposed to decipher."[41] The answer is to be found, Daix declares, in this very idea of an identifying code, with its refusal of abstraction. It would be the coded entry of these little mustaches or drawer pulls that would counter the various nonobjective readings of cubism, by which artists from Mondrian to Malevich to Kupka would redescribe the import of Picasso's and Braque's analysis as a matter of, say, the free-floating colored plane or the schematically allover linear grid. Picasso's refusal of such an interpretation was thus even more emphatic than his dislike of photography. Rejecting any description of his own cubist pictures as abstract, he clearly loathed the idea that cubism should be thought of as "nonobjective" art, just as he hated the notion that it had, on the other hand, spawned the mechanical strategy of the readymade, as it had been developed by Duchamp and Picabia.

Always jealous of Apollinaire's attention, Picasso could not have been pleased by Picabia's reception in 1913. Nor could he have welcomed the spectacle of Picabia entering 291—where Picasso himself had had the only one-man exhibition during the entire time of his cubist production—with a manifesto for abstract art trailing behind him, only to leave it in 1916 with a full-blown doctrine of the mechanical in art and thus art's photographic destiny. During the war years, after all, *291* was one of the few active sites of the avant-garde. Now Picasso's place as leader, secure in the days of *Camera Work*, had been suddenly usurped by Picabia. Indeed, the November 1915 issue would tell the story in four graphic pages: a Braque collage on the cover, a Picasso drawing from late 1912 on the back, both serving as strangely marginalized endpapers for the center two pages on which Zayas's calli-

gramme "Elle" is paired with Picabia's mechanomorph *Voilà
ELLE* (Fig. 26), sharply etched and glitteringly percussive. For
Picasso, looking at this sequence, looking at Picabia's aggres-
sive rendering of the pipes and tubing and bolts and guy wires
of this female-as-erotic-turbine, in the waning days of 1915,
it must have seemed like a portrait of himself as "vieux jeu."[42]

It is necessary, then, to expand one's image of Picasso's
situation in the opening months of 1916 beyond the narrow
range of what Cocteau knew of the avant-garde. For if Cocteau could condescend to the cubist still lifes as old hat, the
stylized realism of theater decor was not their only alternative.
The avant-garde had moved on in the early teens and was
now lying in wait for cubism. It had other tricks up its sleeve,
not the least of which was pure abstraction on the one hand
and the photomechanical conception of art—in which the
readymade combines with the photograph—on the other.

It is to Benjamin Buchloh that we owe the most developed
analysis of the symbiotic relation between abstraction and
photography during the second decade of the twentieth century. Far from forming an opposition around the contrasting
poles of their strategies of depiction—one antimimetic, the
other triumphantly representational—these two ways of
working set in motion, at the level of their mode of production, wholly parallel changes in the technology of the image.
For both photography and abstraction involve a radical "deskilling" of the artist/producer, a flight from the traditional
beaux-arts techniques into the mechanically produced
photographic negative on the one hand and, on the other,

the automated execution of an abstract painting, as, for example, with a pencil and ruler or—even more radically—a roller.[43] And, as a corollary to this deeply impersonal, mechanical fabrication, both abstraction and photography accommodate themselves to the industrial condition of serialized production. If the photographic image is notoriously a function of multiple prints spun out from a single negative, the structures arrived at by abstract painters—the grids, the nested squares, the monochromes, the color fields— are themselves submitted to the mark of the multiple. For the matrix within which any given abstract idea is consummated has been the extended, repetitive production of the series.[44] The logic of abstraction, no less than of photography, is, then, a fight against the unique, the original, the nonreplicable.

And the fatefulness of Picabia's having swum into Picasso's field of vision in that summer of 1915 is that Picabia could be seen to be an avatar of just this combination that would, indeed, form the structural logic of the advanced in art well into the rest of the century. What is crucial to see here, however, is that the threat Picabia represented was not simply an avant-garde position repugnant to Picasso and *external to cubism* but a position that represented to its "inventor" what was *internal* to his creation, even though it could be neither accepted nor admitted by Picasso himself. It is this character of the internal threat that makes the model of reaction formation particularly apposite, not only accounting for the quality of total reversal that Picasso's rejection would take—a reversal that characteristically works from what is considered debased

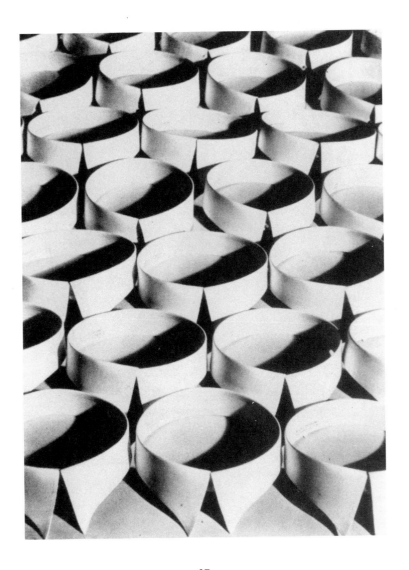

27.
Hein Gorny, *Untitled*
ca. 1930

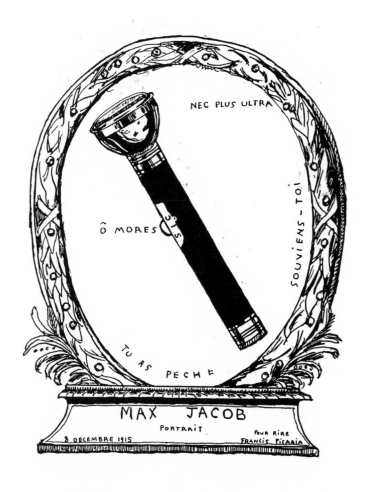

28.
Picabia, *Portrait of Max Jacob*
December 8, 1915

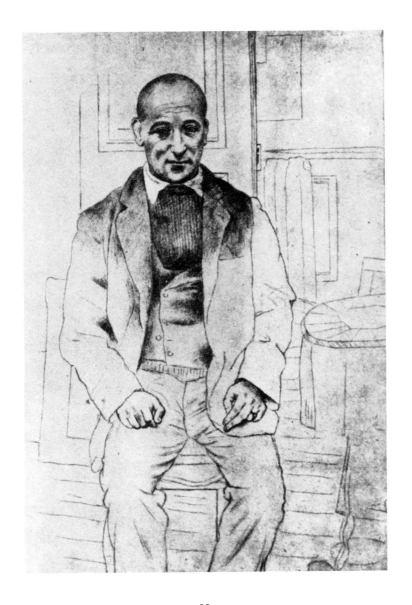

29.
Portrait of Max Jacob
early 1915

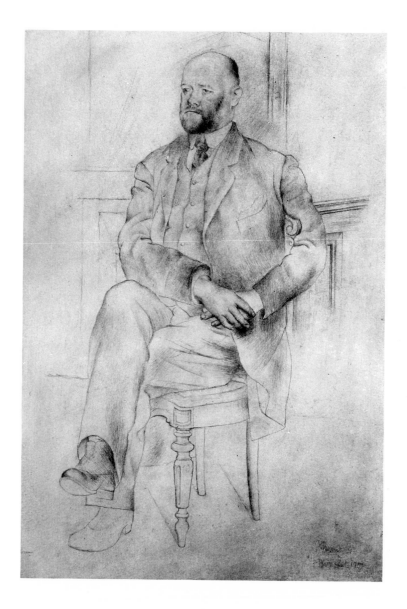

30.
Portrait of Ambrose Vollard
1915

to what is understood to be elevated, indeed sublimated—but accounting as well for the resistance this form of rejection will take once the reactive structure has been put into place. It cannot be stressed enough, then, that the difference between this endogenous model and the usual art-historical notion of external influence is that Picabia's role here is not that of a source but rather of a toxin, the mere trigger for a chemical change the components of which were completely internal both to Picasso's work and to his relation to the historical fate of his own creation.

Thus, beyond what Picasso might or might not have thought of Picabia's talent, Picabia was a harbinger.[45] From a letter Max Jacob sent to Picasso in March 1917, envisioning the collection of his prose poems as *Le cornet à dés*, we get a sense of the troublesome presence of Picabia in the landscape. "I am going to make a publication without any typographic histrionics," Jacob promises, "very simple Kahnweiler-style. I have a horror of Ozenfant chi-chi, etc. . . . and of all Picabiesqueries."[46]

This "horror" Max Jacob voices seems to have been relatively recent; at least it postdates his own collaboration with Picabia in the pages of the January 1916 *291*, in which, having written a text on "La vie artistique," Jacob receives a mechanomorphic rendering of himself as a flashlight, thus having become the subject of, precisely, a "Picabiesquerie" (Fig. 28). But such a complicity with Picabia had been possible then, before Picabia's taunting of Picasso had become open and unabashed in the columns of *391*. Now, as Jacob solicits Picasso for an etching to serve as the frontispiece of his forth-coming book, his understanding of the lay of Picasso's feathers and what will and will not ruffle them registers in his letter. Undoubtedly reacting to the "Picasso Repentant" broadside, Jacob is being careful in early 1917 to denounce Picabia and the mechanomorph.[47] That the mechanomorphic strategy, fully in place by August 1915, had *already* made its troubling portent felt, however, was not something Jacob could have been expected to have known.

Yet on Picasso's part there is a marked difference between the portrait of Max Jacob, made in January 1915 as a com-memoration of his friend's baptism, and the Vollard portrait executed eight months later, in August. The former is still identified with Picasso's recent fascination with Cézanne's *Seated Smoker*, a figure he had explored in both cubist and relatively realist terms throughout the summer of 1914 in Avignon and into the fall and winter in Paris. Cézanne's pres-ence for Picasso is registered in many ways at this time, not the least of these being the tiny picture of an apple that Picasso makes for Gertrude Stein for Christmas as a consolation for Leo Stein's having split their collection and removed his Cé-zannes to Florence. And preoccupation with Cézanne con-tinues into the first weeks of the New Year; it is the seated smoker, in his peasant garb, hands posed on his knees, staring out at the viewer from his perch on his straight-backed chair, that can be felt in the portrait Max Jacob himself described as making him look "like my grandfather, an old Catalan peas-ant"—an identification that also connects the work back to

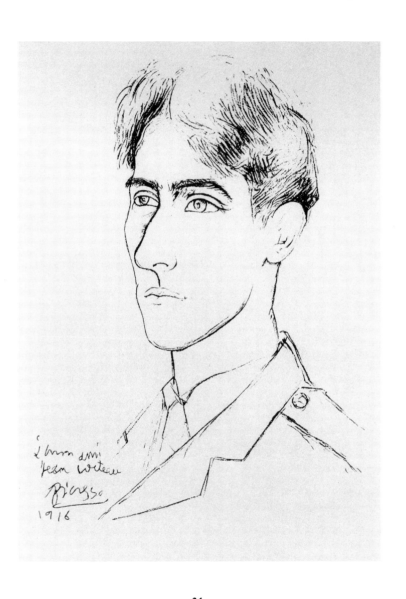

31.
Portrait of Jean Cocteau in Uniform
1916

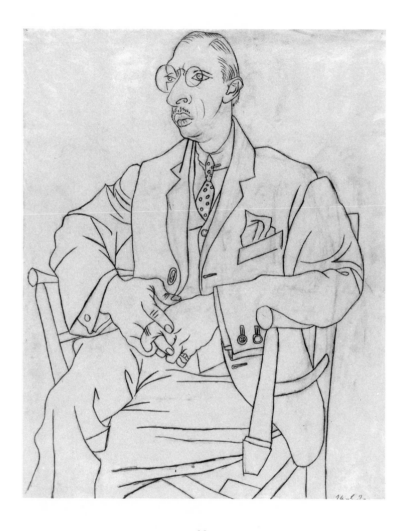

32.

Portrait of Igor Stravinsky

May 24, 1920

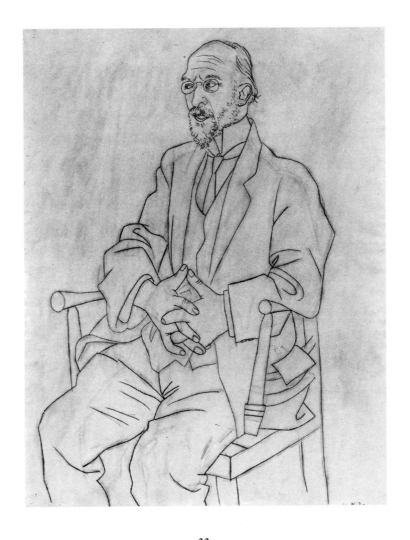

33.
Portrait of Erik Satie
May 19, 1920

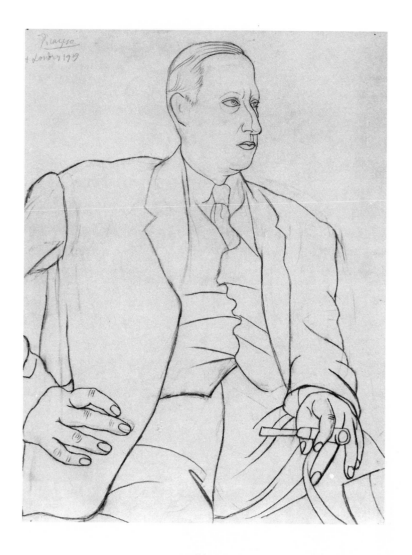

34.
Portrait of André Derain
1919

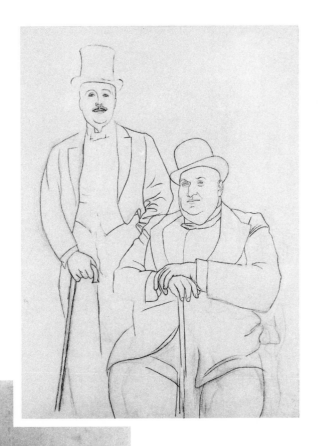

35.
*Serge Diaghilev and
Alfred Seligsberg*
(after a photograph)
1919

36.
*Photograph of
Diaghilev and Seligsberg*

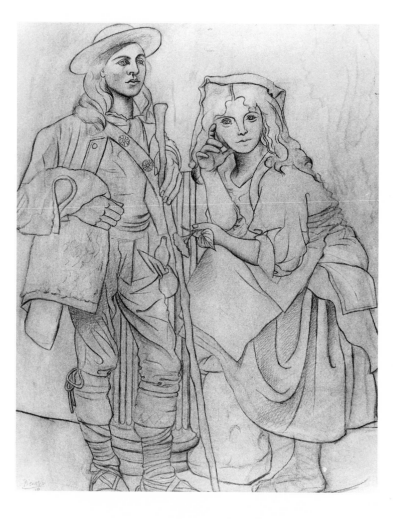

37.
Italian Peasants (after a photograph)
1919

Picasso's own Gosol peasants and the very beginnings of his play with masks.[48]

Thus while Ingres can clearly be recognized in certain of the formal strategies of the January 1915 portrait of Max Jacob, he is not the exclusive preoccupation he would become in the portrait of Vollard in August. There, along with the new formality of both the pose and the setting—the clutter of the studio that serves as Max Jacob's background now changing to the grand interior of so many Ingres subjects, backed by carved wooden paneling and sleekly reflective mirrors—the hardening of the line is unmistakable. At the material level this is the result of Picasso's taking up the steely graphite pencils of the neoclassical draftsman; at the level of the image, it is a function of the increased uniformity of the stroke itself. And it is this hardened line, encasing the bodies of subsequent sitters with its ever more emphatically thick, uninflected contour, stiff and sinuous at the same time like a stubbornly continuous wire, that will become not only the medium of the series of "Ingresque" portraits that Picasso will continue to produce into the 1920s but the matrix of his practice of pastiche.

It is this line—made as though by someone who never lifts his hand from the paper—that serves to trace the contour of the classical nudes that begin to appear in 1918 (Fig. 38), as well as the Corot-based Italian peasants (Fig. 37), the copies after Renoir from 1919 (Figs. 39–41), and the groups of ballerinas themselves based on publicity photographs (Figs. 42 and 46). This line, with its "classicizing" cast, is what performs the famous synthesis of the French masters to which Daix likes to refer, a synthesis based on the recognizable repetitiveness of the calligraphic mark itself: its slowness, its resoluteness, its perseverance. Thus from Poussin, to Corot, to Renoir, to the photograph, the line orders this heterogeneous production into one continuous series, a force of organization that, in bending the various elements to its own will, raises them onto a newer, purer plane, thereby sublimating them. But even while doing so, the serial quality they now take on works to automate the various subjects and to mechanize their rendering.

For Picasso's line now imbibes the robotic character of a mark made in the course of tracing, a line that is so slavishly indebted to the model lying below it that it has lost any connection to the draftsman's own distinctive hand. It is such an experience of the mechanical that will, on the one hand, mark the "second-degree" condition of pastiche, the fact that the artist's relation to the image is always mediated by another proper name, another author. On the other hand, the mechanical will penetrate the "cultural" network of interartistic associations to descend to the industrial base of production exploited by Duchamp in the early teens and insistently disseminated by Picabia's illustrations of Haviland as a desk lamp (Fig. 43) or the American girl as a spark plug (Fig. 25): the ground at which the automation of drawing takes the form of the motley "dumb" outlines of the mechanical draftsman's rendering of the industrial object—the line as invariant, the line as intended for mass production.[49] It is Picasso's line itself,

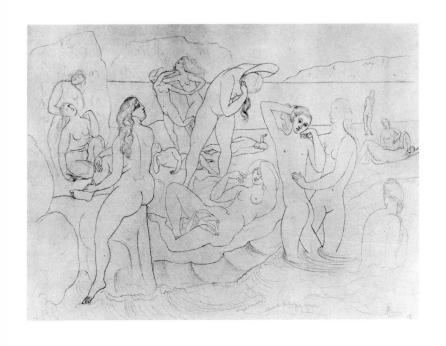

38.
Bathers
summer 1918

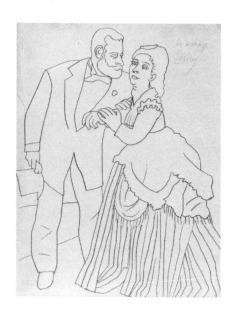

39.
The Sisley Family,
after Renoir
late 1919

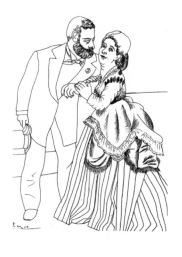

40.
The Sisley Family,
after Renoir
late 1919

41.
The Sisley Family,
after Renoir
late 1919

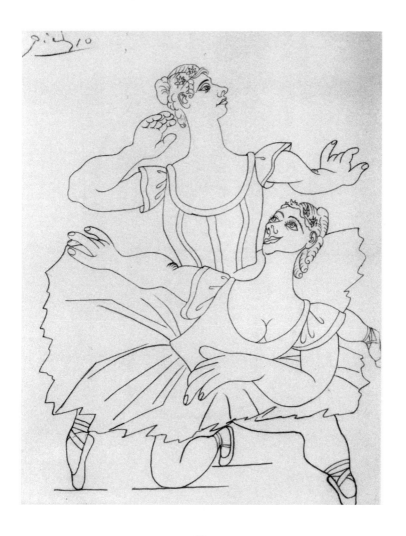

42.
Two Dancers
summer 1919

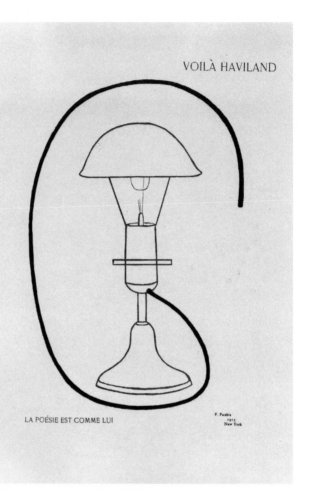

43.
Picabia, *Voilà Haviland*
1915

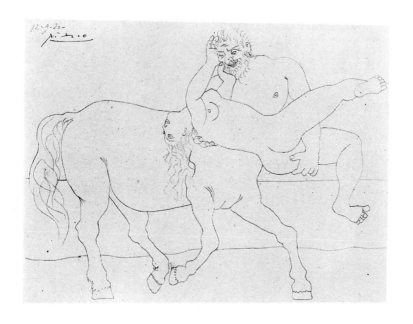

44.
Nessus and Dejanira
September 12, 1920

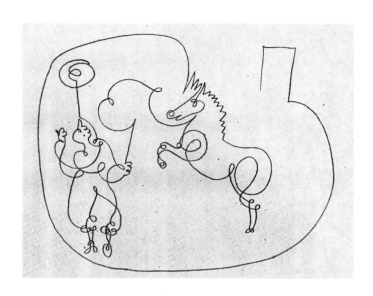

45.

Horse and Trainer

November 23, 1920

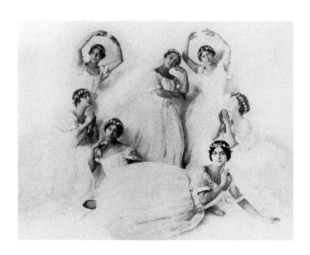

46.

Publicity photograph for Ballets Russes on their New York tour

1916

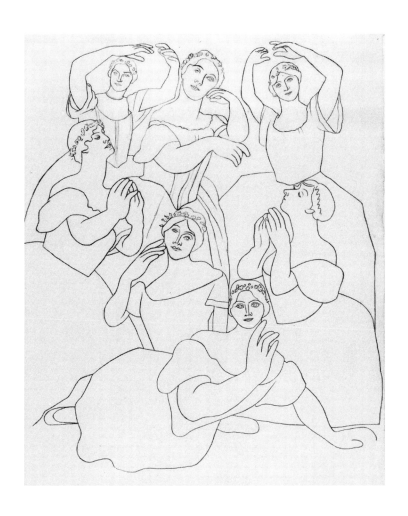

47.
Seven Dancers
(after a photograph with Olga Kokhlova in foreground)
1919

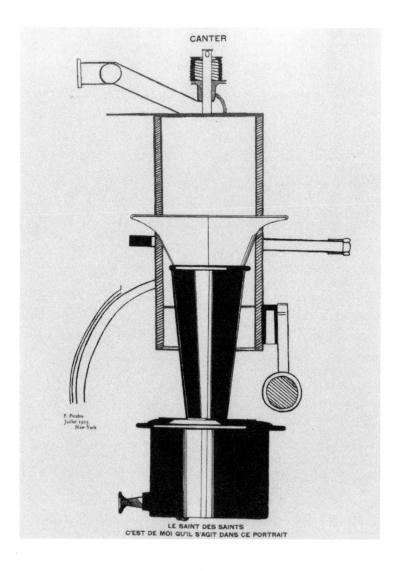

48.

Picabia, *Le Saint des Saints*

1915

then, that ties the knot linking the manufactured object and the pastiched image, revealing them both as simply two orders of readymade.

Further, it is in the meshes of this knot that we recognize the operations of reaction formation. Picasso's supposed classicism, so clean, so pure, so effortlessly productive, is the underside of mechanization nastily taking command. Thus, from the depths of this dialectical relation, in which opposites are inextricably bound as the two faces of the same reality, the very signature of Picasso's virtuosity is branded by the mark of art's deskilling. For that feature of his calligraphic magic—his capacity to spin out intricate anatomical contours without lifting his pencil from the page—carries the mechanical production of the contour, in the form of tracing, as a kind of disease with which it has already been infected. Not only is it there in the modality of the line itself, so mockingly resistant to the shifts and swells of traditional drawing's attempts to make contour responsive to volume. But it also seems to control the very form Picasso's "neoclassical" style will go on to take, as the bloated, disarticulated quality of a figure's hands and fingers, for example, or the staring, abbreviated set of its eyes appears to have its roots in this brutally summary quality of a drawing made as if by tracing.

The "neoclassical" rendering made by copying a publicity photograph of ballerinas symmetrically grouped around Olga (Fig. 47) is not only a perfect example but, placed side by side with any Picabia portrait from between 1915 and 1917—*Voilà Haviland*, for example, or his self-portrait, *Le*

Saint des Saints (Fig. 48)—yields striking similarities in the character of the touch, the insistence on frontality, the compulsion toward symmetry, and the sense of the frozen immobility of the inorganic object. For Picabia, the readymade functioned as an unexceptionable substitute for the sitter: the idea of individuality having been swallowed up by the mechanical conditions of modernity, the singular identity of the portrait subject could easily be reduced to a vanished being for which the mass-produced object was now the acceptable token or sign. For Picasso, this would have seemed an impossible, even repugnant, step. So much so that one might even venture that his sudden commitment to portraiture was in direct opposition to the position Duchamp and Picabia were then beginning to occupy, the portrait being thought by Picasso as precisely that genre in which the image is understood to be transparent to a unique sitter who anchors the representation in the real world.[50] Yet the layers of mediation to which Olga is submitted in this copy made after a photograph of her attest to the distancing that will occur, in spite of himself, in all of Picasso's portraits during these years, portraits whose similarity of handling, pose, lighting, composition gives them the appearance of having been serialized, spun out mechanically, as it were. And indeed, nothing could register the deindividuated character of these effigies so well as Picasso's 1919 portrayal of Massine (Fig. 51), in which the supposed neoclassicism of the treatment is invaded by the quality of photographic shading—not unlike that of the Montrouge self-portrait—to produce the strange graphic hybrid that to this day characterizes the kitsch, photo-based, stereotyped style of sidewalk portraitists.

By the mid-1920s someone like Ozenfant will make exactly the same synthesis between mechanical drawing and classical "purity"—a purported classicism that will have as its generative subject an array of bottles and wineglasses and pitchers wrought by mass production (Fig. 52). Ozenfant will rationalize his decision to take these implements as the nexus of his classicism by calling them *"objets types"*; but the fact that they are the prototypes of multiples produced in the millionfold betrays the connection between automation and a classicism that cannot by this point in time be called a style but must instead be termed a form of "styling." The styling that settled in as the hallmark of mid-1920s *rappel à l'ordre* was, however, the particular blend that Picasso had already fashioned in 1916–17, in the grip of reaction formation against classicism's supposed opposites. And it is this character of a line not so much drawn as styled that generates the strange paradox of this draftsmanship—namely, the extraordinarily depersonalized feeling of the line to which the name of Picasso will henceforth be attached.

The Picasso literature is mute on this subject. It does not seem to notice, any more than Picasso does, the automated, serialized, mechanical character of this line, the way it has— in the name of classicism, purity, and the culture of the museum—come to embody the very opposite set of values. Denial is at the heart of reaction formation and it is to be found in the reception of this work just as surely as it was involved in its production.

And, continuing with the logic through which one's defensive, symptomatic behavior covertly brings into being the very thing one wants to disavow, the relationship between this strangely slavish contour and the modeling that comes in certain cases to swell it into intense relief produces the "photographic" quality of Picasso's neoclassicism, the experience that what we are seeing has been relayed through many strata of technical mediation, being the handmade copy produced by tracing a photograph that has been made of another work, whether antique sculpture or painted image (Figs. 49 and 50). There are many sequences of drawings in which we see modeling coming to inhabit this contour in progressive stages, like the tones emerging on the surface of the photographic print as it lies in the developer. A striking example is the sequence lifted from Renoir's portrait of Sisley and his wife, in which we move from a first drawing of bare outlines, to an intermediary one of tentative hatching, to a final one of determined light and shade (Figs. 39–41); but similar sequences can be found throughout this period. Thus these drawings become the symptomatic acknowledgment of what Picabia had already accused Picasso of in January 1917: that the reality lying now behind the Ingresque mask is indeed the automation of art, of which the Kodak is, in fact, the more than adequate sign.

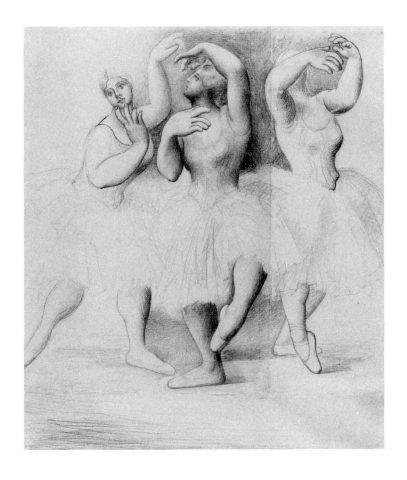

49.
Three Ballerinas
1919–20

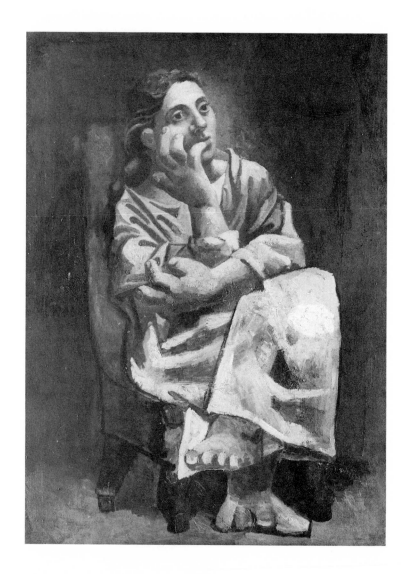

50.
Seated Woman
1920

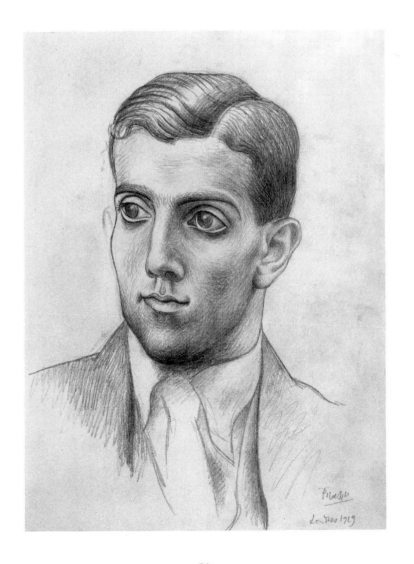

51.
Portrait of Léonide Massine
summer 1919

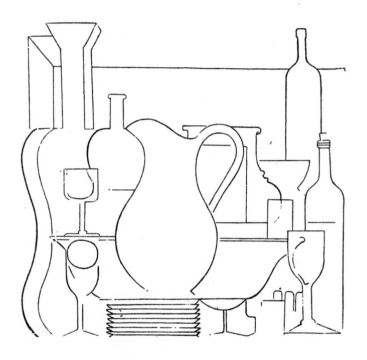

52.

Ozenfant, *Dessin puriste*

1925

• • •

It is spring 1914. Kahnweiler is at the rue Schoelcher examining the harvest of works Picasso has made in a burst of renewed enthusiasm for *papiers collés* after a whole winter of nothing but oil painting. One of the collages, he notices, prominently displays André Level's calling card (Fig. 53), placing the time of the work's execution most probably in February, from the period when Level had been preparing for the fantastic sale of the Peau de l'Ours collection. And indeed it strikes Kahnweiler that something had happened precisely in February to account for this concentrated return to the medium of pasted paper.

Kahnweiler is drawn to three of these works in particular, for they are different in feel from all the rest of Picasso's production, different because of the innocently continuous space of their backgrounds, different because of the play that's been made to fashion an ornate frame for their borders on which to place a fake brass nameplate: a signature so long banished from the front of Picasso's works now making its return in the form of the triumphant tag of the Old Master (Figs. 54, 55, and 62).

Yet no matter how much they strike him as *hors série*, they also seem—two of them especially—to set the tone for the present group as a whole, which appears to be concentrated on the idea of transparency and reflection, light that pierces through objects and light that is itself pierced by being refracted into a range of color. For these two collages (Figs. 54 and 62), employing as their grounds a stretch of stippled wallpaper that Picasso seems indeed to have purchased in February, summon up the specter of neoimpressionism, with its pointillist stroke and its chromatic analysis. And yet, Kahnweiler also has to acknowledge, Seurat's system is produced only to be placed in brackets. For the paper, while it is colorful—a rich mauve, sprinkled with purple and white dots—makes no attempt whatever at the rigorous division of color impressions into their chromatic components. And why should it? The world to which it belongs—that of bourgeois decoration—is miles away from neoimpressionism's aspirations toward a science of light.

Kahnweiler chuckles at the extraordinary wit of one of the collages in which, within its mauve expanse, the dotted wallpaper supports a miniaturized *collage-en-abyme* representing a pipe and a sheet of music on a table, both this tabletop and the side of the fake picture frame, itself built from a strip of imitation molding, casting hypothetical shadows onto the stippled surface. But, Kahnweiler smiles, which surface is it supposed to be? Is it the ground of an indeterminate depth set back within the "frame," the luminous surround of traditional easel painting reconstellated here by means of the divisionist system for transcoding color, a system so conspicuously attached to the name of Seurat but now "signed" by Picasso?

Or, as an alternative to this atmospheric possibility, should the wallpaper be read as the material ground it literally claims itself to be? Is it folding representation over onto reality to produce itself as a framed stretch of wallpaper on which another, smaller picture hangs, paper that is just like that of any wall on which the work might eventually be installed? (And here the background of the next member of the group particularly strikes Kahnweiler, close as its paper is to the wall covering of his own salon [Fig. 55].[51]) Yet if this literalist reading is the one we opt for, then a third possibility rears its head in the guise of a perverse form of illusionism: what we are looking at is not a picture of a picture hanging on a papered wall but a mirror instead. We are looking at the blank reflective surface of an ornately framed looking glass, through which we see, on the opposite "wall," a collage of a pipe and sheet music, decorously hung on a surface onto which it casts a shadow.

And indeed it is this curious telescoping of space between the "real" wall in front of one and the "reflected" wall behind one's shoulders that then cycles back to the opening possibility, that of the Seurat system, of the luminous, atmospheric surround. Cycles back to it even having already mediated it through the competing system of the wall—flat, decorative, artificial—and the reflective bracketing of the mirror.

Kahnweiler notes the presence of the mirror in so many of the collages, with or without the stippled wallpaper, the mirror making itself felt in the molding strips that run vertically behind many of the objects—indicating the carved edge not so much of table or chair rail but of a gilded frame holding another picture or, more likely, a mirror—or still again in the rays of shadow and light that cup these objects like so many reflections, or in the use of rhymed materials to equate glass surface with glass object, the transparency of goblet or compote dish with the shine of the mirror.[52] And indeed, Kahnweiler makes a note about one of the collages (Fig. 58), which he would then carefully copy into the album of photographs his gallery keeps of Picasso's work: "*verre, pipe, carte à jouer sur une cheminée*," he writes,[53] it probably being the case that the mantelpiece of Picasso and Eva's new apartment on the rue Schoelcher is surmounted by the inevitable mirror.[54]

If one imagines Kahnweiler being alert to this departure that takes place in the spring of 1914, it is because it was Kahnweiler, after all, who was particularly sensitive to the way color had been consistently recalcitrant to cubism's analysis of the pictorial system. If Delaunay had thought he could sneer in a letter to Kandinsky, written late in 1912, that "the Cubist group of whom you speak experiments only in line, giving color a secondary place, and not a constructional one," in Kahnweiler's eyes it was Picasso's and Braque's very strength that they had rationalized their analysis of representation by seeing that problems of form could be solved only by separating them off from problems of chroma.[55] Accordingly in "The Rise of Cubism," he would explain that Picasso "had to begin with the most important thing, and that seemed to be the explanation of form, the representation of the three-dimensional and its position in space on a two-dimensional surface. . . . The question of color, on the other hand, was

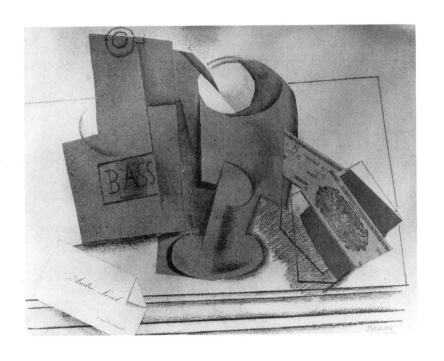

53.
Bottle of Bass, Wineglass, Packet of Tobacco and Calling Card
early 1914

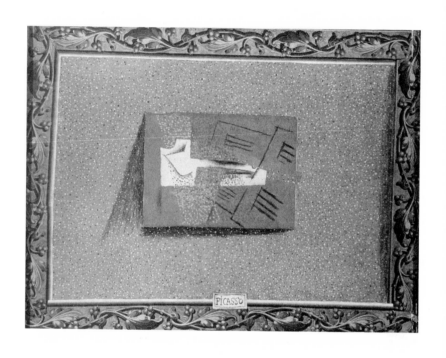

54.
Pipe and Sheet Music
spring 1914

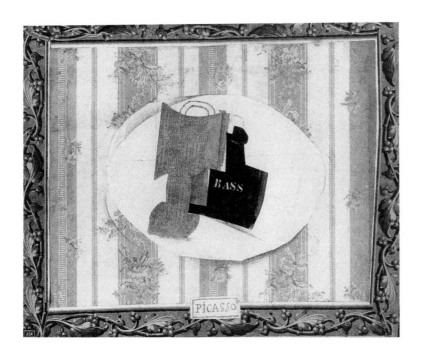

55.
Glass and Bottle of Bass
spring 1914

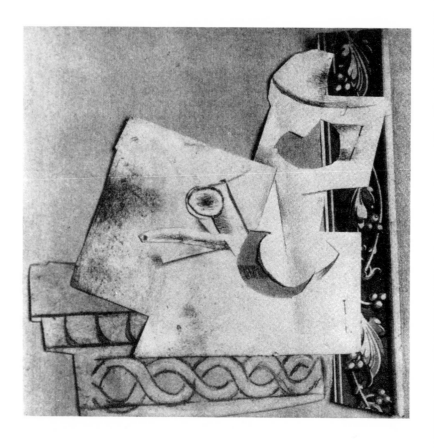

56.
Pipe and Wineglass
early 1914

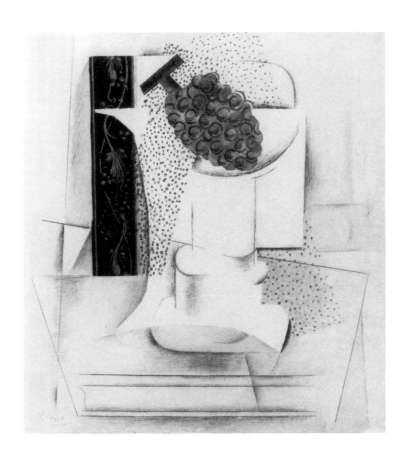

57.
Fruit Bowl with Bunch of Grapes
spring 1914

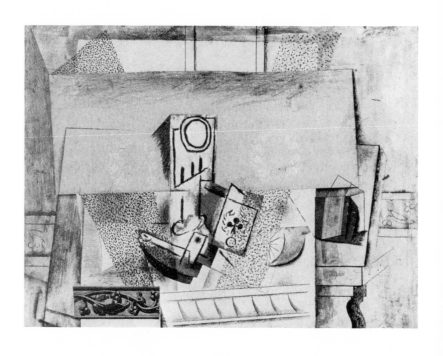

58.
Glass, Pipe, Playing Card, on a Mantelpiece
spring 1914

completely by-passed." And to illustrate this dilemma further, Kahnweiler adds: "Several times during the spring of 1910 Picasso attempted to endow the forms of his pictures with color. That is, he tried to use color not only as an expression of light, or chiaroscuro, for the creation of form, but rather as an equally important end in itself. Each time he was obliged to paint over the color he had thus introduced."[56]

But if color had been banished from the development of cubism, it has often been remarked that it returned automatically, as it were, with collage.[57] The collage elements, being themselves shards and fragments from the world of real objects, are endowed with local color, "local color" being the painter's term for the actual hue of a given object, unmodified by the effects of light and shadow (termed: modeling, chiaroscuro) or of aerial perspective (dimming and bluing color as an effect of distance). This undiminished color was, as Kahnweiler points out, something the cubists had had to suppress during the time when they could admit colors into their work only as a function of chiaroscuro, so that the umbers and ochers and olive greens and grays that appear in their hermetic pictures are not the colors of the objects they are depicting but rather the display of light and shadow across the shallow relief of their surfaces.

Collage put an end to this monochrome laboratory. Colored papers, wallpapers, product labels, matchboxes, tobacco pouches, calling cards—all bore their own coloration in tones that were decidedly local, in the painter's sense of the term.

And indeed, Kahnweiler ratified the effort Picasso and Braque devoted "in the years from 1910 to 1914 to the reproduction of this 'local color.' "

There are two problems, however, in this story of the return of color to cubism through collage's automatic recourse to the "local." The first is that, statistically speaking, collage remained by a very long way an affair of browns and grays and beiges. Newsprint did nothing to disrupt this monochromy, nor did Braque's persistent use of wood-grained paper. And Picasso's own choice of commercial wallpapers, running as it did to florals and stripes and decorative patterns for the most part in rusts and tans, did little to break the grip of a palette still devoted to the issue of spatiality and relief and quite resistant to the intervention of areas of intense color into this organization, an intervention that could only bring its own disruptive counterpoint into play.[58]

The second problem is not statistical but conceptual. Cubism had engaged in a dismantling of the conventions of representation so that each element in the building of a three-dimensional illusion was first made to appear on its own, unsupported by the object it was presumably depicting, as patches of modeling, for example, lay about the picture surface like so many rumpled fragments of an exploded balloon. With the onset of collage, these elements were further transformed into a series of semiotic equivalents so that even the iconic immediacy of analytic cubism with its direct appeal to touch was now mediated by the flattened sets of signifiers for the various pictorial signifieds, such as *depth, light, texture, shape.*[59] Should we be tempted to add color to this list, the conceptual pitfall is that while every other element in the representational system can be mediated by a set of equivalences that present us with the self-evident experience of the substitute—something that is even true of texture as Picasso and Braque experimented with a wide variety of surfaces like gesso and sawdust-impregnated paint to signify the distinctly different surfaces of wood and glass, or as they used floral wallpapers as the signifiers of the grained wood of musical instruments—this is not true for color. Color remains local, the colored surface of a given object and thus the unmediated color of the thinglike plane itself beaming its way directly from the canvas to the perceptual apparatus of the viewer.[60] And if we say that, to the contrary, there are collages in which color is unlocalized so that first a blue fragment and then a white fragment and then a black one work in alternation to support the designation of the musical instrument, this delocalization has precisely the effect of a retreat from color and a move backwards toward the idea of tonality as chiaroscuro, color as modeling, color as cast shadow, that had been its fate within analytic cubism.

That Picasso, in particular, *wanted* to open cubism to color, and that from the beginning of his collage activity he acted from time to time on the assumption that the new system of analysis might allow this, is clear from the paintings he made beginning in the winter of 1912–13, in which he set about translating the lessons learned in the school of collage into the greater permanence, scale, and stability of oil painting.[61] One of these is quite fascinating in that it appears to attach itself to the series that began in the spring of 1912 with the very first introduction of local color into analytic cubism—the painting *Notre avenir est dans l'air*—and continued into August 1912 with the Sorgues *Landscape with Posters* (Fig. 59). This painting, *Female Nude: "J'aime Eva,"* from the autumn of 1912 (Fig. 60), combines the use of large, flattened, overlapping rectangles with the appearance of intense color, as the various planes of the figure's head and body are filled in with nearly unmodulated stretches of red, blue, yellow, and green. The extreme arbitrariness of this color in relation to the "real" colors of the human figure indicates that Picasso's initial analysis turned on a redesignation of the idea of local color, displacing it from the surfaces of the natural world to the wholly factitious veneers in the world of cultural artifacts. Benjamin Buchloh has focused on the *Landscape with Posters* as an example of Picasso's early sense that it was here that he would find an answer to the recalcitrant problem of the analysis of color.

Writing that "color was so highly invested and over-determined, even in its most advanced scientific status within Neo-Impressionism, that none of its options was literally accessible to the Cubist project [during the analytic phase]," Buchloh then contends, "when [color] comes back into Cubism, it is linked to mass culture and material surfaces," the significance of which is that from the chromatic point of view such surfaces are profoundly arbitrary.[62] This arbitrariness, which removes color from a system of resemblance, connects

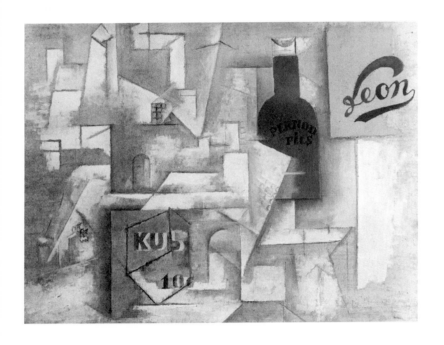

59.

Landscape with Posters

summer 1912

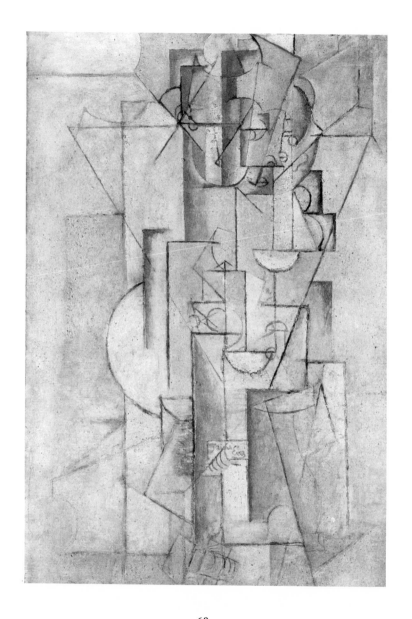

60.
Female Nude ("J'aime Eva")
autumn 1912

it to the condition of convention, in the sense that a product label, for example, is not chromatically tied to anything but the caprice of the manufacturer. The intense pink of the "Léon" billboard from *Landscape with Posters* is thus, semiotically speaking, deeply unmotivated—which is to say, disconnected from the color of any natural thing—becoming instead the arbitrarily determined chromatic sign of the hatmaker for whom it serves as commercial insignia. In this sense the color of the product label, functioning as a ready-made conventional sign, dismantles the iconic condition of local color and converts it into a level of semiotic transformation (based on arbitrariness) that would seem to parallel that of the other elements of the collage universe.

"J'aime Eva," however, is not only an unfinished painting but something like the closing out of a series rather than the beginning of a new one in which an ever deeper mastery of the semiology of color could unfold based upon the substitution of arbitrary local hues for natural ones.[63] Why this should not have been the direction Picasso would choose to pursue is unknown. What is obvious, however, is that it was the option taken by Léger, the artist who was most busily and vociferously focused on the world of billboards and urban advertising at this moment and who had, by the winter of 1912–13, shifted his own vocabulary over to what he called "contrasts of form," by which he meant a pictorial structure of impacted, tubular, humanoid shapes filled in with the stridently arbitrary colors of red, blue, and yellow. It could be that Léger's having staked his early claim to this territory made

it unattractive ground for Picasso himself to investigate. But from what follows in Picasso's work, it is likely that his hesitation was more a function of the conceptual problem that, no matter how arbitrary a given color is in relation to its presumed referent, the mere fact that it continues to perform as local color binds it seamlessly into the homogenous surface of the oil-painting system. Which is to say, these colors— arbitrary or not—have no way of declaring their apartness from the pictorial surface and thus no semiotic leverage on the world of representation. They are, that is, colored surfaces rather than the *signs for* colored surfaces. And it could even be said further, in criticism of Léger's assumption that red, blue, and yellow would deliver the image over to the arbitrariness of the industrial world and thereby break the grip of nature, that within the pictorial system to which his curving planes are now integrated, nothing could be more "natural" than the classical palette's traditional declaration—from Poussin, through David, and even into Millet—of the primary colors, red, blue, and yellow, as painting's conditions of possibility, and thus its very nature.

In any event it seems clear that in his efforts throughout 1913 to translate collage into oil painting, Picasso didn't feel he had the means to recreate the semiotic thrust of collage at the level of color. That it might be recreated at other levels is a function of the way Picasso attempted to hold on to the heterogeneity that had been imposed on the surface of the work of art with the invention of collage.[64] Oil painting is a medium of supreme homogeneity, suspending pigment in a uniform viscous medium that itself becomes an analogue of the uniformity and continuity of the space within which the world's objects set themselves out for display. Collage disrupts this homogeneity both on the literal level, as a miscellany of different things actually assemble on the picture surface, but also on the semiotic level, as the added collage piece functions as a miniaturized substitute, or sign, for the surface of the work as a whole.[65]

If the discreteness of figurative plane from its supporting ground is necessary to the oppositional structure through which the very idea of representation was being reworked by Picasso, then it was not an easy matter to translate collage to oil paint and canvas. Indeed, the heterogeneity that Picasso labored throughout 1913 to produce on canvas involved a conception of the oil painting as itself a matter of zones that were not so much discontinuous as in upheaval, so that areas of the field seemed to swell into relief, to visibly cover over the supporting surface, and even to cast a shadow back onto that background. The coffee grounds, sawdust, and sand that Picasso mixed into his paint in order to work certain areas up into a kind of rough stucco facade, as well as the planes he built up out of gesso or of the plastic skin of Ripolin enamel, recreate the experience of a plane that is covering over or occluding another surface, one for the *absence* of which the plane itself now serves as "figure."

The simulation of shadow cast by these areas of relief became the object of its own developing repertoire as the obvious signifiers—such as velvety passages of modeling or opaque black shapes—were augmented by the use of news-print planes (as in the cast shadow of the decanter in *"Au Bon Marché"* [Fig. 8]), the "normal" function of which, in Picasso's collage practice, had been to create the signifier for *light* and *transparency* rather than their absence. In the winter of 1913–14 both Picasso and Braque added another element to this repertory, or rather reverted to one that had been actively employed during the period of high analytic cubism, when chiaroscuro had been applied in passages of shading that were not so much gradated as stippled in a kind of monochromatic version of Seurat's divisionism. Entering initially as a modality of shadow, stippling becomes a resource for Picasso throughout that winter and into the opening weeks of 1914, one that, while it is still related to the overall monochromy of collage, begins to define large planar areas in a kind of doubling of the earlier use of newsprint.

It is at this point, sometime in the first months of 1914, probably by February, that Picasso suddenly switches stippling over from the monochromatic registers in which he (and Braque) had been employing it and reconceives of it in terms of divisionism—which is to say, in the mode of chromatic analysis; and it is with this new function for the pointillist mark that Picasso finally opens collage and cubism itself to the full embrace of color. It is because this yield to color in all its decorative implications was to be so decisive in reorienting Picasso's relation to cubism as a whole (in the eyes of many of his critics this embrace proved to be a kind of death grip in which the seriousness and rigor of cubism itself finally perished), that it is important to attempt some kind of model for what happened at this juncture—whether we read its occurrence as a triumph over the problem of color or a fateful succumbing to its attractions.[66]

The model I want to develop turns, indeed, on *Pipe and Sheet Music*, coming as it does from the beginning of Picasso's new series of collages and making use, along with five other works, of a stippled mauve wallpaper that, once it fell into Picasso's hands, must have struck him with the force of a triumphant "Eureka!"[67] For it is this wallpaper, I would argue, that brought with it a resolution to the color problem that is both stunningly simple and strangely complex.

In the world of aesthetic activity surrounding cubism in late 1913 there were many claims being made for divisionism, most particularly by Delaunay and Severini, both of whom were asserting that the cubist gains in a new conception of space could now be carried out on the basis of chroma alone. "Simultaneous contrast," taken over directly from Seurat and his still-active apostle Signac, became the basis for the constructive laws that Delaunay had referred to in his letter to Kandinsky. And as Delaunay further explained, the dynamism of color relationships, in acting directly on the human sensorium, produces the possibility for a painting purified of the extraneous clutter of depicted objects. "I have found the laws of complementary and simultaneous contrasts of colors which sustain the very rhythm of my vision," he had said.

What this means is not only that divisionism had entered the discourse of advanced art as a way to formalize pictorial construction and thus to move it toward complete abstraction but that "simultaneous contrast" invoked the very form of retinal stimulation that switched color over from localization in the surfaces of objects to a kind of direct bombardment of the human perceptual apparatus: each point of color the index of a ray of light striking the eye. It is this very claim to visual directness and unmediated intensity that made pointillism absolutely unusable for Picasso, except where, in restricting it to tones of gray as a mock sign of chiaroscuro's shadow, he could deploy it ironically, brushing color against its own grain, as it were.

But suddenly this mauve wallpaper, mechanically stippled in purple and white, went further than brushing color against the grain. In the resplendence of its surface vibrating with a kind of ersatz chroma, it produced the experience of color itself, but color now bracketed as sign, color mediated through the mechanical processes of printing, color produced in terms of the secondhand condition of the copy. This was not the divisionist immediacy of the color point as index of retinal stimulation—for indeed there is no attempt to follow the divisionist analysis of light into color complementaries. It was instead the reworking of the divisionist mark in conjunction with the color plane to transform it into a signifier: not the sensation of color but the sign for color. What Picasso could now see was that color could be made available for cubism through this commercially produced mark of the secondhand, the mediated, experience already bracketed as copy.

Indeed, this may be why the mirror enters the repertory of

collage elements at this point, since the mirror's doubling produces spatially what the mechanized surface of the wallpaper produces in terms of chroma, namely, the experience of indirectness, of relay. And further the mirror produces a profound ambiguity in the reading of the mock-divisionist beams of light, since we cannot tell if these are supposed to be "real" sunbeams, entering the space as though through a window, or the ersatz of light rays produced by the gleams of reflection cast across the surface of a mirror (Fig. 58).

In all of this Picasso is, of course, on cubism's familiar ground of a flattened space activated only by the sign's marking of depth. But the problem of the mauve wallpaper, making it a kind of Trojan horse smuggled within the walls of cubist analysis, is that it is the very medium of cubism's enemy, an enemy in the form of ornament. With the Nabi painters' love of these very wallpaper patterns for pressing relief out of the space of the painting, for example, or with the Fauve worship of the "pure arabesque," the flat plane understood as a supremely decorative element had entered the space of modern art.[68] It was this decoration that cubism disdained. As Kahnweiler had said—speaking of such painting's debasement as a desire "to be 'decorative,' to 'adorn' the wall"—"Picasso perceived the danger of lowering his art to the level of ornament."[69]

In locating ornament as "low" rather than high, Kahnweiler is signaling what could be called the internal dialectic of the avant-garde in the opening decade of the twentieth century, a dialectic Clement Greenberg sets up as a simple binary or antinomy in his essay "Avant-Garde and Kitsch."[70] The idea that the avant-garde found its very identity in defiantly segregating every aspect of its practice from the chromolithographic prettiness and the petit-bourgeois easy taste of kitsch has already been challenged as too simple by Tom Crow, who has argued that cubist collage followed Seurat's early interest in poster art and the socially marginal types of cabaret entertainment it advertised, by prospecting in the fields of mass culture both for cheap, industrialized materials and for a typographer's process of composition. It was only by gaining access to the commodity in this form, Crow reasons, so it could be deployed against the rigidified, mandarin traditions of high art, that the commodity itself could become an emblem of both artistic and social freedom.[71]

To Greenberg's oppositional structure and Crow's model of critical recoding, however, there has to be added a third paradigm, one that acknowledges the presence of kitsch deep within the highest aims of the avant-garde to the extent that in the years 1910 to 1914 every radical formal move could be felt to have been already compromised by a connection to the pervasiveness of kitsch culture. Such a paradigm, according to which it is the enemy inside that must be identified and extirpated rather than an external enemy that must be opposed, would be dialectical. And this dialectic is nowhere clearer than in the two separate historical strands that braid together around the term *decoration*. On the one hand, there is the aesthetic tradition of the Nabis and Fauves. On the other, there is the culture of the commodity: not the one

pertaining to the paraphernalia so often identified with collage—the wineglasses and carafes and pipes and newspapers
of the working-class café—but rather the one of bourgeois
home decoration, with its wallpapers and fringes, its doilies
and bibelots, and above all its entirely anodyne commercial
language, the advertising posters and labels and calendars and
fancy packaging, processed through the seductive forms of
what was then called "modern style," which is to say, the
popularized and mass-produced version of art nouveau.[72] This
commodification of the decorative had its Parisian temple in
department stores like the Bon Marché, as it had as the high
priests of its visual language such commercial "geniuses" as
Adolphe Mucha and Eugène Grasset. That Grasset was the
author of the influential *Method of Ornamental Composition*
(1907), tying him to Beaux-Arts processes of instruction, is
symptomatic of the linkages between the aesthetic and the
commercial strands of decorative practice.

It was Matisse himself who expressed consternation at the
way the chromatic wing of the avant-garde kept being over-
taken by the commercial palaces of decoration, to produce in
these artists an unwonted experience of complicity with the
vulgarization of the "ornamental." Accordingly, he says:

> Finally, after the rediscovery of the emotional and dec-
> orative properties of line and color by modern artists,
> we have seen our department stores invaded by mate-
> rials, decorated in medleys of color, without modera-
> tion, without meaning. . . . These odd medleys of color

and these lines were very irritating to those who knew what was going on and to the artists who had to employ these different means for the development of their form.

Finally all the eccentricities of commercial art were accepted (an extraordinary thing); the public was very flexible and the salesman would take them in by saying, when showing the goods: "This is modern."[73]

Matisse is not simply describing a confusion that could be perpetrated on the uninitiated, with the implication that for "those who knew what was going on" these strands of high and low would be held separate. He is also saying that the "artists who had to employ these . . . means for the development of their form" received them already corrupted as kitsch. And the presence of this dialectic can even be seen in the paired pictures through which Matisse developed first a Cézannean version of a given theme and then a flattened, primitivizing, arabesque-driven decorative one—pairs such as the two *Sailors* (1907), the two versions of *Le Luxe* (1907), and the two *Dances* (1909 and 1910). In each case the second version, with its thickened reddish contours both pulling the internal surfaces of the figure taut and vibrating against the flattened color of the surrounds, takes on the very optical flicker that Matisse was to disclaim for his art and, in so doing, produces as a kind of afterimage the posterlike experience of the detested modern style.

In Picasso's case, the adoption of the stippled wallpaper at the beginning of 1914 as a means of "breaking through" to the mediated color sign brought with it, as one of its corollaries, what might be called the "decorative *un*intentionality" of modernism.[74] For the condition that the mauve paper carried of the duplicitous, of an Other that produces the false double of one's self or of one's intention, once again marks a point of complicity between advanced art and its kitsch counterfeit. As Picasso explores this terrain of the decorative through the spring and summer of 1914—with increasing overlays of ornamental surfaces and textures, as well as the continuing use of the mirror and the decision now to produce painted copies of the wallpaper surfaces he had until then applied directly to his works with scissors and paste—he seems to be confident that he can control this invasion of cubism by the ornamental enemy. But one can already feel the emergence of anxiety about the confusions that exist within this simulacral world, through the suddenly restored act of affixing a signature, of pointing to high art's refusal of the anonymity of the decorative by giving a proper name to the Seurat system even though that name is now "Picasso."

This, we could say, is the first, tentative example of the moves that would come to install the reaction-formation structure within Picasso's work. In one stroke, the kitsch attractions of ornament are warded off and resublimated by the affixing of a proper name. But here as well, the paradoxical logic of reaction formation is in operation, as the symptom secretly performs the activity against which it is the supposed defense. Because in evoking the divisionist system through which Seurat believed he had produced a scientific, positivist rationalization of real visual experience, this wallpaper also betrays the way Seurat's art had already been delivered over to the decorative during his very lifetime: to symbolist ideas of evocative color-perfume; to the art nouveau embrace of Henri Van de Velde and *les XX*.

This twist—in which the decorative evokes the proper name whose invocation is then expected to rescue the work from the vice of ornamentation, which, however, has already stolen inside the proper name itself to vitiate its authority— gathers momentum in Picasso's work during the summer of 1914 in Avignon, as the First World War was about to ignite. It is thus not surprising that there was another name to which Picasso was drawn that August, one whose "signature" was more complex than the easily recognized formula of juxta- posed color dots.

The figure in question was Ingres, whose hallmark could be said to be the formal portrait—the single figure seated close to the edge of the picture, filling the canvas with the curves and countercurves of his or her sumptuously clothed body, a play of ornate frames within frames, of which there were sev- eral repeated "signatures," including the frequent use of a mirror to close off the space behind the sitter by producing a ghostly replica of his or her corporeal presence and the me- ticulous rendering of ornamental fabrics, whether confected as the clothing worn by the subject or as the covering of the walls of the depicted interior.

Several of the still lifes Picasso worked on in Avignon pro- duce these characteristic features of the Ingresque setting,

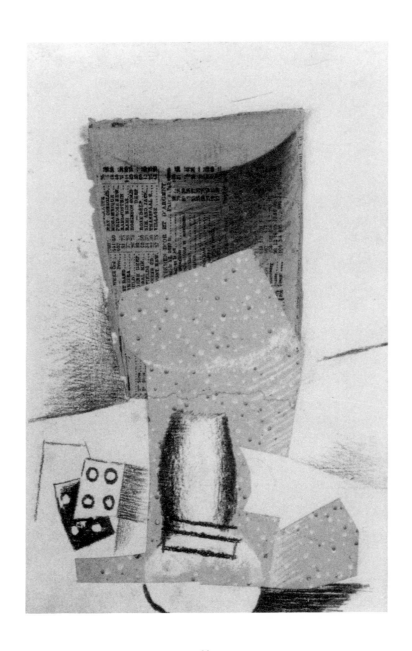

61.
Wineglass and Dice
spring 1914

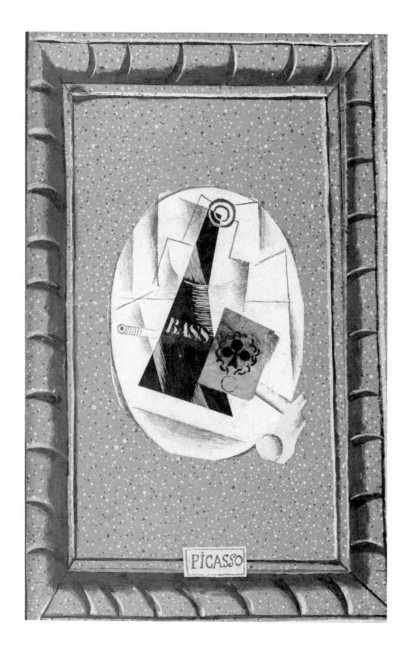

62.
Bottle of Bass, Ace of Clubs and Pipe
spring 1914

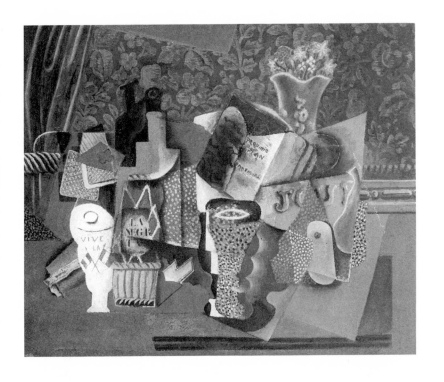

63.
Playing-cards, Wineglasses and Bottle of Rum ("Vive la France")
summer 1914–15

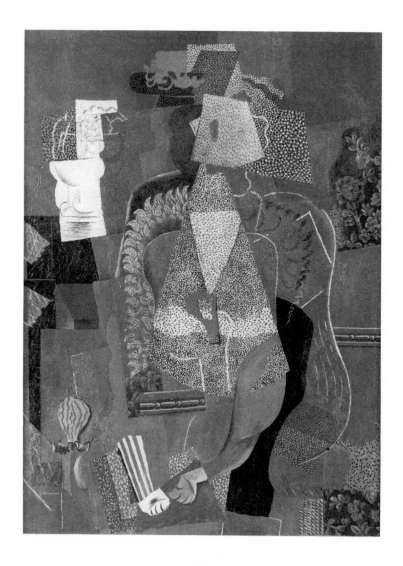

64.
Portrait of a Young Girl
summer 1914

making the presence of a mirror behind the assembled objects more overt than it had been in the Paris collages of the spring. In the *Green Still Life* (Daix 778) Picasso works on the reflective sheen of the mirror, while in the still life referred to as *"Vive la France"* (Fig. 63), the handpainted facsimile of a stretch of wallpaper vies for attention with the decorative panoply of objects illuminated by divisionist dots.

But the name "Ingres" implies the portrait. So it is not surprising that Picasso should attempt a large-scale picture designated on its reverse side as, simply, *Portrait of a Young Girl* (Fig. 64) but redolent on its face of all the qualities of Ingresque production. The nests of concentric curves are there, as the figure is embraced by the rhymed patterns of the chair back, the wreath of a feather boa, and her own self-encircling arms. The painted reproduction of ornamental fabrics is also a necessary component. But there is the suggestion as well of a mirror forming the background for the sitter: not only felt in the way the minute details of the boa to the left of the body are summarized in a ghostly, simplified version on her right—the photographic negative, so to speak, of the positive rendering of their substance—but also seen in the "negative" reduplication of the compote dish that appears to be perched on the marble surface of what might be a mantelpiece.[75]

If I am right about this picture—as well as its accompanying still lifes—then Ingres does not make his first appearance in Picasso's work of the midteens through the medium of a classicizing style of drawing or mode of portraiture. Ingres enters cubism itself in the way the semiology of color—the solution to how to produce a sign for chromatic experience that will not simply instantiate the sensation of color as such—insisted on indirection or mediation. This Picasso sought in a play of decorative surfaces that itself seemed to call for the presence of a mirror in order to signal the optical relays and proxies and doubles that the polka dot produces as color's "sign."

· · ·

The exhibition that was to startle Uhde so, convincing him and others that Picasso had abandoned cubism for the assumption of a wide range of historical styles, was nonetheless composed in large part of cubist pictures. Of the over one hundred works exhibited at Paul Rosenberg's in October 1919, twenty-five were part of the series representing a still life set before an open window, a sequence of works begun in Saint-Raphaël that summer that came collectively to be called the *Balconies*.

This theme, which Picasso was to continue throughout the winter, eliciting in the end some 125 objects—drawings, pastels, gouaches, prints, even little sculptural models—generated the kind of frenzy of concentration and production associated with one of Picasso's major paintings: the *Demoiselles d'Avignon*, for example, or *Guernica*.[76] But in this case there was no "major painting." Perhaps the most elaborated of the works is *Still-life in Front of an Open Window at Saint-Raphaël* (Fig. 65), a gouache that measures only 35.5 × 25 cm (14 × 10 in.).

One Picasso scholar, commenting on the sprawl of the series of studies and the absence of a central work for which they might have served as preparation, insists: "The number of such images hardly matters. What matters is the group as a whole; the group constitutes the work itself."[77] And this "work," accomplished by this repetitive spinning out of the theme, is generally agreed to be a "dialectic between Cubism and Classicism," a dialectic that imbricates these two styles, seemingly so opposed to each other, into a continuum that braids cubist space through the *veduta* opened by the window. Or, as Daix would put it, the *Balconies* achieve a structure "in which Cubist space reverberates to an infinity of sky and sea."[78]

Dialectic has, of course, been the leitmotif of what I have been presenting here, the logic that undergirds the structure of reaction formation. But dialectic is a term that ceases to function without a sense of the necessary, internal relationship of the two terms it pictures as both falling apart and coming together. And in what Daix proposes of the *Balcony* series, namely, that it is a consummation of a "marriage between the Cubist revolution and Renaissance perspective," there is to the contrary a peculiar aura of nonnecessity, a sense of the arbitrariness of this couple, almost as incongruous as Picasso's marriage to Olga.[79]

If the *Balcony* series *is* in the grip of a dialectic, however, and this seems to be the case, it is the struggle of cubism with its mechanical, automatist Other, not—as it seems on the surface—of cubism and classicism. In Picasso's practice, classicism, as we have seen, is merely the sublimated face of a more powerful and threatening force, the automation of art through the linked logics of the photomechanical, the readymade, and abstraction. And if Picasso acted phobically against the idea of automation, deskilling, and serialization—erecting the defense of classicism, uniqueness, and virtuosity—this was not because the mechanical was simply an external threat to cubism but rather because it stood as a logical conclusion that could be drawn from within.

For this reason it is interesting to observe that the Saint-Raphaël series has as its most continuing element not the open window—which is absent in many of the works—but the cubist guitar, which serves as a kind of transducer for both the space of each individual work and the series as a whole. Structured by a spatial idea for which Picasso went so far as to fashion several cardboard sculptural models (Fig. 66), the instrument is basically formed from the intersection of two planes: a single, guitar-shaped piece wedged horizontally into the sheet from which it was cut, the sheet itself set vertically to act as a fin that slices the instrument into two symmetrical halves. It is this fourfold mirroring structure that then forms the core from which all further spatial elaboration will exfoliate, whether onto the "infinity of sky and sea"—seen through the windowlike cutouts opened within the structure itself—or into the figure/ground oscillations of a more properly cubist interchange.

But in being the engine that generates the series, this little stereometrical model, with its vertical fin from which the horizontal figure is suspended, continually reworks the idea of

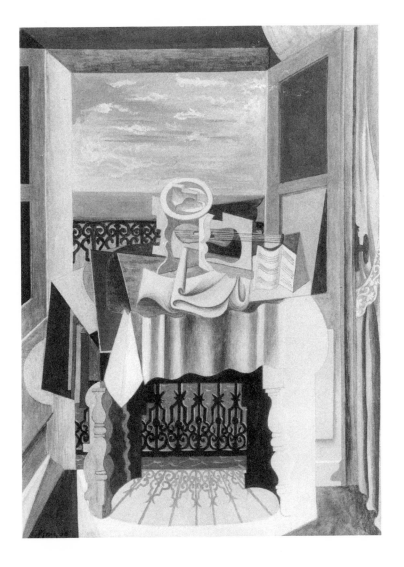

65.
Still-life in Front of an Open Window at Saint-Raphaël
1919

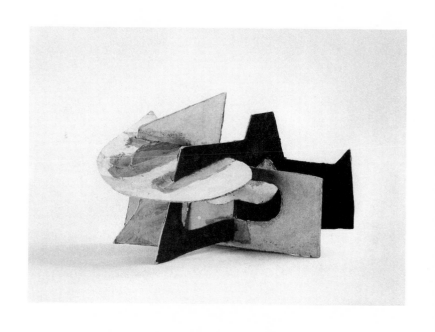

66.
Compote and Guitar
1919

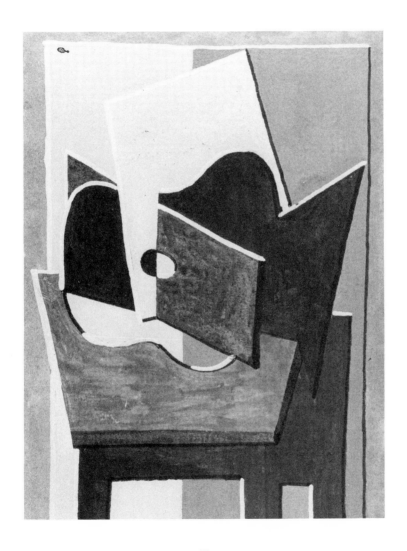

67.
Guitar on a Table
November 24, 1919

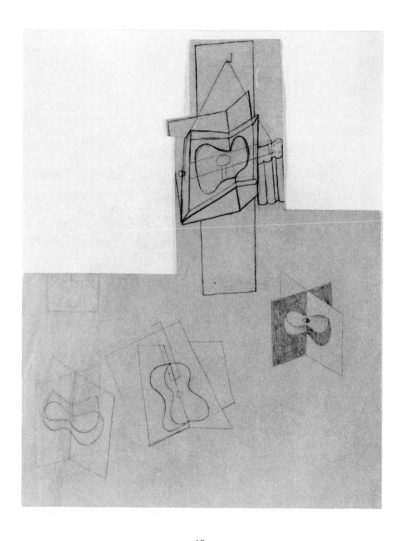

68.
Five Studies of a Guitar
autumn 1919

the mirror, the fin functioning as a plane behind which the objects on *this* side find themselves doubled or as a supporting ground within which real space is reflected in the form of a simulacrum (Figs. 67 and 68). It has often been remarked that in this series, in which Mediterranean light and salt air seem to come flooding into cubism, nothing could be less securely "natural," since the curtained opening Picasso envisions is often clearly that of a theatrical stage. And further, since the window itself is frequently shown shut, its panes reflective rather than transparent, the basic image to which the series seems again and again to revert is even simpler than that of the still life arranged in front of either window or proscenium. Rather it is that of the cubist setup placed atop a mantelpiece, whose mirror generates the objects' doubles even while capturing the reflections of the surrounding space.

At no time in its past, even with the funny plays with the little fractured dice in 1914, had Picasso's cubism been a matter of this stereometric transection, with its dumbly mechanical symmetry.[80] But the mirroring capacity lodged at the heart of the little sculptural object now becomes the very model of the automaton: generating form simply by doubling, setting up the conditions of serial repetition through the idea of successive reflections, deskilling production through the very simplicity of the structure itself.

That the little stereometric model would become, in the hands of self-styled "constructivist" sculptors, the very basis for *abstraction* in sculpture—Naum Gabo explaining in the 1930s how, by the late teens, this formula had been "discovered" as the principle of all three-dimensional form, like a kind of Euclidean statement from which to generate the cubes and spheres and polygons that inhabit real space—demonstrates the way the lessons of cubism were often read by others as leading to the nonobjective in art.[81] Treating the spatial principle of cross-axial construction as an algorithm capable of spinning out repeated variations on a basic formula, "constructivist" practice, whether in the hands of Gabo or of Max Bill, organized itself—as had much abstract painting—in terms of serial production. And indeed, the constructivists took it as a given that the rationalization and generalization of form should accommodate itself to, even become the very basis of, the mechanization of production within the age of advancing technology.

The Saint-Raphaël series thus assumes that very character of defensive mimicry we've seen in other parts of Picasso's work at this time. For, even as it produces a mammoth refusal of what others saw as implicit in cubism, the means for generating abstract planes to be set in formal relation to one another—a refusal that summons to its side lushly modeled color, obsessively realist detail, the boring of deep vistas into space—it imitates the form of abstraction in its very embrace of the idea of the series as, indeed, "constituting the work itself." And within this series, it is the cubist-guitar-turned-stereometric-model lying at the heart of all the variations that becomes the very embodiment of the abstraction Picasso was intent on rejecting.

As a consequence, what mechanical drawing had done to

Picasso's line in his pastiches of Ingres and Corot and Renoir, the automatism of the stereometric mirroring now does to his own relation to cubism. These still lifes condemned to repeating, as though by compulsion, the self-same elements from the cubist repertory—the guitar, the compote dish, the sheet music, the gueridon—lose the gorgeous sense of improvisation the choices had possessed during the prewar years. Instead, as they steadily take on exactly the character of fetishized relics Cocteau had accused them of being, these still lifes emerge as pastiches of cubism, cubism itself now automated and serialized.

Picasso had a long history of having been labeled a *pasticheur*. From the reactions against the Rosenberg show, back to the abusive hysteria in 1914 over the high prices modernism achieved in the Peau de l'Ours sale, Picasso had lived with this accusation. In 1914 he was called "the imitator Picasso who, after making pastiches of everything and finding nothing more to imitate, perished in his own Cubist bluff," an epithet reminiscent of the assessment of his very beginnings in 1901 as a "brilliant newcomer" in whom "many likely influences can be distinguished—Delacroix, Manet (everything points to him, whose painting is a little Spanish), Monet, Van Gogh, Pissarro, Toulouse-Lautrec, Degas, Forain, Rops. . . . Each one a passing phase, taking flight as soon as caught. . . . Picasso's passionate surge forward has not yet left him the leisure to forge a personal style."[82] He was even accustomed to applying it to himself in the early days, as when Salmon reports him offering to take some German visitors to the

Lapin Agile to see the painting he identified as "from his Lautrec period."[83]

But cubism, Picasso had truculently told his Russian detractors, was his, what he invented, what so deeply bore his mark that at its height he had not even felt the need to sign it. Speaking to Brassaï in 1944, Picasso casually casts off all the work leading up to cubism as just so many "isms," so many successful hostages to public taste, made to give him the space to do what was original to him, what was authentic. "It was the success in my youth," he says, "that became my protective wall . . . The blue period, the rose period, these were the screens that shielded me. . . . It was in the shelter of my success that I could do what I wanted, everything I wanted."[84]

Financial success was not enough, however, to protect Picasso from the message delivered to him by the fate of the avant-garde in the early teens: that the implications one could legitimately draw from cubism—that were indeed already being drawn from it—were ones Picasso himself found unbearable. And yet by a logic that operated outside what he could consciously control, his own art began by 1915 to assume exactly those features he wanted to disavow, although the form by which it took on their mantle was of course purified, heightened, sublimated. Pastiche of others as well as of himself became the vehicle of this sublimation. And in this peculiar turn of events in which Picasso begins to act as though two separate stylistic matrices—cubism and classicism—were optionally available to him, his relation to *both* seems equally dissociated, equally unauthentic.

It is at this junction that Picasso invents a formula for imitating or pasticHing what we could call "the phenomenological preconditions of stylistic authenticity,"[85] namely, the sense of an author behind the work, an author with all the unplumbable depth and resonance of his or her personality and thus the indelible individuality of that subjective ground from which the work is drawn—"as unique and inimitable as your own fingerprints." The sense of how to instill this sense of authenticity—no matter how miragelike—came, I would warrant, from that branch of Picasso's practice in which his recourse to pastiche was far more in evidence than in his contemporaneous rehearsal of cubism.

In analyzing pastiche, Genette reminds us that its practice is not a purely stylistic affair; the thematic material of the model is also in question. Style, being a matter of form in general, comprehends "both the form of expression *and* that of content. For example, in Tolstoy, a certain conception of charity; or . . . with Dostoyevsky a certain obsession with crime; or with Stendhal, the link between spiritual life and refined places; or with Hardy, geometrical vision."[86]

With Ingres—we could continue this analogy—the thematic material is portraiture. If in his neoclassicist fervor Ingres labored over history painting and mythology, his abiding genius, the concern that made his work most unalienably his, was for the portrait. And it is in the drive toward the portrait—which Picasso spins out into fantastic variations, as he captures the features of his sitters with his mechanical stroke but also renders faces from the photographs that fell into his hands—that Picasso will attempt to reproduce the content of his neoclassical model. Yet the woodenness and impersonality of these portraits also reveal that this content was leaking away even as the repetitiveness of their serial production tried to regenerate it.

Here, however, in the very idea of portraiture, Picasso found a way to stamp his work with the mark of authenticity. For it is at this point that Picasso set off down the road of *concealed* portraiture, turning everything—mythological scenes, commedia dell'arte tableaux, even still lifes—into hidden records of his own persona, the smuggled-in evidence of his presence as authorial subject to the objects represented in his art.[87] Indeed, in one of his largest and most flagrant early pastiches, a *Return from the Baptism* (1917–18), the specific scene he selects to copy from Le Nain in the style of Seurat (Fig. 69) could easily have been motivated by his own participation in the baptism of Max Jacob, for whom he had served as godfather—making this yet one more example to add to the growing list of concealed self-portraits. But whether or not the artist's own proxy is included in a given work—in the figure of Harlequin, for example—the strategy of concealed portraiture always turns on the idea of the narrative of the artist's life as a way of evincing his commitment to the norm of the authorial subject, even while the work continues to operate in the modality of pastiche.

Thus there need not be a full-scale (self-) portrait—such as the triumvirate from the *bande à Picasso* hidden in the 1921

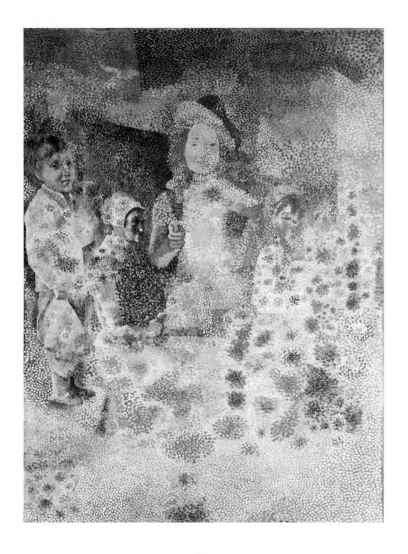

69.
Return from the Baptism, after Le Nain
autumn 1917

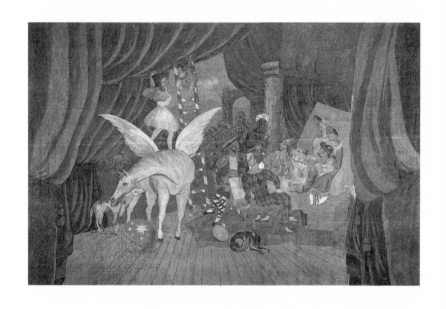

70.
Parade Curtain
1917

Three Musicians or the shadowy figure who enters *The Milliner's Workshop* (1926 [Fig.71]) to project Picasso's self-
reproach at the time of Gris's death—secreted within the
work.[88] These figures need not even be present, since the idea
of self-presentation can now be applied to the work simply
through the vehicle of the diary form, as Picasso methodically
begins to date every piece of his production, noting not only
the day but sometimes the hour of its creation.[89] And further,
in conformity with the notion of subjectivity as divided into
a manifest surface and latent depth, the diary itself is understood as a medium of extreme secrecy, available to an audience only by being written in cipher. Referring to Picasso's
simultaneous recourse to overtness and concealment, Daix
thus writes: "In 1932, right in the middle of his Marie-
Thérèse period, [Picasso] confided to Tériade, 'work is a way
of keeping a diary,' an admission which seems all the more
perverse because Picasso was at pains to keep his codes secret
and played on misunderstandings."[90]

Although Picasso's passion for stealth extended to every
corner of his life—he and Sabartès were accustomed to com-
municate with each other concerning even the most ordinary
transactions in a code so devious that, Françoise Gilot reports,
each was often at pains to know what the other meant—it
was the Marie-Thérèse affair that represented the greatest and
most elaborated of his secrets. From 1927, when he made her
his mistress, through 1935, when she bore him a child, up to
the winter of 1939–40, he kept her locked away as an enigma

that repeatedly billowed forth on his canvases and in the pro-files of his sculptures but that even his closest friends didn't fathom as a person who actually existed.

It is assumed, of course, that Picasso had no choice but to hide Marie-Thérèse away. She was, after all, underage: only seventeen when they became lovers. And further there was Olga's restless and increasingly hysterical jealousy, which made secrecy the order of the day.

But what is strange about the complicity of all of Picasso's biographers with his explanations is that Picasso's supposed fear of Olga's discovery doesn't square with the artist's famous independence, not to mention his reputed sadism, and the fact that the minute he felt like breaking with Olga, which is to say the day he lost interest in Marie-Thérèse, he had no trouble at all informing his wife of his mistress's existence and arrang-ing for a separation that would leave his various studios and apartments to himself. Further, the fact of Marie-Thérèse's status as a minor needs to be examined in the light of his claims that secrecy was imperative. For the relationship was maintained as illicit for fully ten years *after* she ceased being underage; second, her mother seems consistently to have been Picasso's willing ally in his liaison with her daughter, making legality more or less irrelevant; and third, and most important from the point of view of the *structural function* that conceal-ment seems to play in Picasso's work, the very *fact* of her minority, and thus the alibi for secrecy, may have been one of the things that attracted him to her in the first place.[91]

Indeed, during the 1920s, as Picasso was fusing the idea of

concealed self-portraiture and painting-as-diary to create an equivalent of the private resources of subjectivity, he must have desired some kind of ballast for this allegory of selfhood. The daily tracking of a secret life, or of a life *as secret*, was the already developed formula into which he folded Marie-Thérèse, making it unsurprising that he should subsequently choose to spell out their connection in a succession of visual "novels"—the word is Pierre Daix's—each panel carefully dated as to month and day.[92]

These romances, illustrating the life of the sculptor with his model, and the scenes from the *Rescue* series (1933), through which the story of their relationship bubbled up from its real-life hiding place into the circuit of his art, gave his work a new kind of urgency. And, interestingly, it was Sabartès, having returned to Picasso's life in 1935 after the separation from Olga, and necessarily privy to this mystery, who maintained that the meaning of his master's art would be found when one learned how to crack its code. In this way, he promised: "We would discover in his works his spiritual vicissitudes, the blows of fate, the satisfactions and annoyances, his joys and delights, the pain suffered on a certain day or at a certain time of a given year."[93] One would discover, that is, something like the phenomenological subject: the individual who is fully present to himself.

Picasso had long since discarded any notion of such an individual as the author of his own work. His repeated testimonies (to Brassaï and others) that he had nothing in mind when he started a work and, further, that he was not person-

ally responsible for the course it took are avowals of this ab-
dication. Yet, paradoxically, he liked to say that the elaborate
record he kept of his production, everything carefully stored
away and assigned its proper date, would allow a future generation to reconstruct the entire process of his creation:
"Some day there will undoubtedly be a science—it may be
called the science of man—which will seek to learn about
man in general through the study of the creative man. I often
think about such a science and I want to leave to posterity a
documentation that will be as complete as possible. That's
why I put a date on everything I do."[94]

Here, then, is "selfhood" strangely projected as a form of
documentary: to be packed in a time capsule and found at a
later date, when it would be discovered not just by those
others who did not witness it at the time but *by its own "agent"*
as well—the peculiarly "absent" subject who also did not
witness it. For Picasso, even the diary's testimony does the
work of pastiche, as dissembling and mimicry become the
medium of his art.

DIME NOVELS

YOU ARE A NOVELIST AND YOU HAVE DECIDED, FOR whatever reason, to write a biography of Picasso. Because you subscribe to the view—which some are now calling "canonical"—that Picasso's art issues directly from his life, you are confident that the biographical project will open effortlessly onto the aesthetic conditions of his "genius."[1]

Being a novelist, however, you are not interested in repeating what you regard as the shapeless accounts of the master's experiences so often recorded by other scholars: Picasso's succession of mistresses, wives, studios, pets, courtiers. What you want instead is to wrest a "character" from this successiveness and to thrust this personage into the path of his fate. What you need to plot is that moment when a man either goes forward to meet his moral challenge or, shrinking from it, cheats some important part of himself of its destiny. Given what you believe to be the continuity between your subject's art and his biography, you are not sure whether to track this moment through the seismographic record of the work or to seek it in the various accounts of his daily existence. But you are sure that if you find the climactic moment in the story of the life, the effects on the art will be apparent.

Let us say the novelist in question is Norman Mailer, who indeed has declared the literary nature of his intentions in the very title of his book, *Portrait of Picasso as a Young Man*.[2] The story you tell would then concern a character far more troubled than the usual legend of Picasso's almost God-like capacities would suggest. Your Picasso has to be dragged, screaming, to school as a boy. Your Picasso is a short, girlish adolescent, whose claim to prowess has to come from the power of his pencil, his ruthless ability to draw. This is the young man whose desperate poverty keeps driving him back to Spain after brief forays to Paris and whose depressive reaction takes the color blue and lasts four long years. But this is also the Picasso who has tasted enough of fame and attention that, rather than endure the distraction of caring for his closest friend, he cuts him loose, speeding him along the path to suicide.[3] This is, in short, the genius who is skating over very thin emotional ice but doing extremely well until the fateful day in September 1911 when, brought before the Paris magistrate in connection with the theft of the *Mona Lisa*, he looks at Apollinaire, who is being held for questioning in the case, and says to the police: "I do not know him."[4]

Here, you say, is the cave-in, the collapse, the succumbing to "primal panic," the ultimate failure of nerve. A man rats on his best friend; he will never be able to take some part of himself seriously again. Picasso, Mailer writes, "is now obliged to see himself—a clown searching for machismo who looks to fire his pistol at three in the morning through the roof of a cab. Small wonder if his harlequins were sad. They knew how he would act in a crisis" (337). If we need to find proof of this puncturing of his self-respect, then, says Mailer, "the evidence is in his work." For he sees Picasso as having just enough in reserve to keep going through the fall and winter of 1911–12. After that it's over. By the spring of 1912, Picasso "is a painter again, decorative, agreeable, charming." He becomes a "Synthetic Cubist," which is another way of saying that he reduces cubism to nothing more than decor. "Synthetic Cubism is to Analytic Cubism," writes Mailer, "as Formica to walnut" (340).

Given this plot, it might be tempting to retort that this is a book that has already been written, its earlier title announcing even more clearly than Mailer's a triumph and a breakdown. But John Berger's *Success and Failure of Picasso* is about not so much a personal as a social collapse.[5] From its very outset it charts Picasso's rise against a backdrop of European culture and politics: the feudal resistance of Spain to modernity that makes Picasso a permanent "primitive"—what Berger will call a "vertical invader"—even at the center of European industrialized culture; the anarcho-symbolist movement that will sweep the avant-garde up into an ethos of revolution; the carnage of World War I that will then permanently dwarf and thus outmode this avant-garde's "bohemian" forms of outrage; the fact that revolution will now become "inevitably political" (83).

Picasso's "failure," in Berger's eyes, is an inability in the postwar period to find a subject outside himself worthy of the intensity of his emotions. And in the absence of that, Picasso has been left to celebrate his magical beliefs in himself as a "noble savage" digging deeper and deeper into his own isolation. Picasso's idea of a subject is that it is a mere pretext for a bravura performance. After all, the artist insists, when you come right down to it, there are very few subjects. "To invent a new subject," he says wistfully in 1953, "must be wonderful. Take Van Gogh. His potatoes—such an everyday thing. To have painted that—or his old boots! That was really something" (140).

Berger, however, wants to correct Picasso on this issue of subjects as "inventions." If Van Gogh painted new subjects, these were not willed into existence but were "what he naturally found as a result of his self-identification with others." This is the way all new subjects are introduced into painting. Listing some examples—"Bellini's nudes, Breughel's villages, Hogarth's prisons, Goya's tortures, Géricault's madhouses, Courbet's laborers"—Berger then cautions: "All have been the result of the artist identifying himself with those who had previously been ignored or dismissed. One can even go so far as to say that, in the last analysis, all their subjects are *given* to artists. Very few, such as he has been able to accept, have been given to Picasso. And this is his complaint" (142).

The moment of Picasso's failure to accept the subject matter of modernity—redefined politically—occurred in 1917 when Picasso collaborated on the ballet *Parade* (Fig. 70). Berger condemns this work in much the same terms in which Adorno rejected Stravinsky's *Sacre du printemps*. It is, he says, a form of displacement of politics into art. For, claiming to be about "reality," it creates an irrational, frenetic world of shock, isolated against the battles involving real blood then actually raging. Ironically, perversely, the *Sacre* could thus become a form of consolation for its outraged viewers: "The madness of the world, they could say, was the invention of artists!" (89).

Within the isolation produced by this split between the anarchic urges of the prewar avant-garde and a new, organized form of the political, Picasso falls back into his "primitive" position as vertical invader. He dramatizes his status as outsider, as barbarian at the gate, by mocking the center. "It was at this time," Berger writes, "that Picasso first began to caricature European art, the art of the museums. At first . . . he caricatured Ingres" (94). The symptom of Picasso's "failure" thus manifests itself initially in the postwar practice of pastiche.

It would be impossible for Berger to conceive of the rupture in Picasso's art as coming in 1912, with the advent of collage, a moment that brilliantly responds to what he calls "the pressure of . . . the historical convergence which made cubism possible" (83). But then it would be difficult for many other scholars and critics to follow Mailer to such a conclusion since, for most, collage represents a momentous turn in the history of representation, whether read politically, semiologically, formally, or symbolically. These writers are not hostage to the exigencies of plotting a novel, however.

If for over ten years Gide carried around his various news clippings about the counterfeit ring and the teenage suicide pact, waiting for a way to "weld this into a single homogeneous plot," it was because he knew that a modern work could not simply be based on a *fait-divers*, even one as sensational as the theft of the *Mona Lisa*. He knew he would have to find what Apollinaire would call "an internal frame," which is to say, the projection of the outside into the inside of the work so that art and reality would change places and the observer would not know where one began and the other left off.[6] This was the principle Apollinaire saw in collage, with its structural condition of *mise-en-abyme*: a hall of mirrors in which the real—the bit of newspaper—becomes the "ground" for a "figure" that in turn becomes a figure of the "ground." *The Counterfeiters*, with its novelist hero keeping a notebook of the novel he is writing, itself called "The Counterfeiters," is such a collage-made-fiction.

Mailer's plot is both less modernist than Gide's, however, and more personal than Berger's. It shares the penchant for historical anecdote that besets all of Picasso's biographers. It turns, as we've seen, on the moment when, like a boxer entering the ring after having agreed to take a dive, Picasso is supposed to have massively lost face. This is in his own eyes, of course, but also in the eyes that had served for many years as mirrors of his fragile self-esteem—those of Apollinaire and, far more importantly, of Fernande Olivier, his "serious mistress," his equal—"neither a whore nor a playmate, but a woman in his domain" (93)—and his companion in the adventure of "deep sex" (207). Because for this to work as a Picasso plot it would seem there needs to be a woman.

It might have been possible to write the novel on the basis of Picasso's painted record of their love affair, even though this would get increasingly difficult after the advent of cubism and the submersion of Fernande's physical likeness under the barrage of canted facet planes. Even further, the fact that those of Picasso's impassioned attempts to wrest intimacy with a subject from the stuff of cubism that *do* occur during this time are directed not at Fernande but at Daniel-Henry Kahnweiler, Wilhelm Uhde, Ambroise Vollard, Fanny Tellier, and ultimately Eva Gouel would also make this record a rather recalcitrant witness. Looking around for something else on which to plot the intensity of their affair, one would find Gertrude Stein's testimony equally unrewarding. She found Fernande exceedingly limited and took evident delight in recording Picasso's impatience with her as their relationship deteriorated in 1910 and into the spring of 1911. Their public spats and the fact that Picasso spent the summer away from her builds the case for most observers that Picasso's "eight years of boredom" had been coming to an end long before the *Mona Lisa* affair, a conclusion confirmed by the advent in October or November of 1911 of "ma jolie"—who, Daix insists, inspired a far deeper connection with Picasso than Fernande ever had: "When we spoke of [Eva Gouel] two thirds of a century later, tears came to his eyes."[7]

The possibility of plotting Picasso's love affair with Fernande was given a formidable boost, however, by the 1988 publication of her *Souvenirs intimes*, in which Fernande at last broke the silence about herself that she chose to maintain in her earlier *Picasso and His Friends*.[8] Addressing this new book directly to Picasso and claiming to speak from the very heart of their relationship, on the basis of diaries she began to keep as a teenager and presumably continued into the time of her relationship with him, she assures Picasso that she is now undertaking to tell him about her early life so that "perhaps you will understand me better. You always had doubts about me, about my love, about this deep feeling that meant that all of me belonged to you, to you alone" (11).

It is hard, reading sentences such as these, not to be made uneasy; for how, one must surely ask oneself, could Picasso have lived with Fernande for eight years and known nothing of the details of her youthful biography? Could what Picasso "knew" be the same, presumably false, information that Fernande produced for *Picasso and His Friends*—in the telegraphic introduction she titles "Myself"? There she speaks of her middle-class upbringing with her parents, which opened naturally onto a great love of literature and art: "When I first saw the paintings of the Impressionists in the Luxembourg Museum it was a revelation to me. . . . Whenever I had a moment I would escape to the Luxembourg, and this marked the beginning of my abiding love for this sort of painting."[9] This cultural equipment is used to support her claim, which Mailer accepts, that she could be a natural sounding board for the

poetic production that surrounded Picasso, as well as an in-
formed eye for his painting. In her description of herself she
never says what she was doing living at the Bateau-Lavoir,
the ramshackle warren of studios where she had Picasso for
her neighbor, nor does she admit that she had been working
for three years as an artist's model.

Yet Picasso, who was completely aware of her comings
and goings for the year between when they initially met and
when she finally agreed to live with him, was fully cognizant
of those aspects of "Myself" that have nothing to do with the
truth. Are we to assume that he needed to be told that the
people she grew up with were not her "parents" and that her
knowledge of art was as completely primitive as her grasp of
poetry?[10]

For whom, then, is *Souvenirs intimes* being written?

With its tone of wounded self-justification and the phan-
tasmatic character of its story, this curious document comes
across as an elaborate replotting of Fernande's "life" in order
to project two entirely contradictory versions of herself. The
first is of an innocent young girl, virginal until she met the
love of her life, her theoretical intactness being a function of
the frigidity which meant that no matter how many men she
slept with—and since she was an artist's model for the three
years before she came under Picasso's protection, this was a
very large number indeed—she nonetheless remained pure.
The second is of a seductress-in-spite-of-herself owing not
only to a beauty that turned men into beasts but to a volup-
tuary reflex of her own that made her their helpless accom-

plice. Indeed, the traits that Fernande repeatedly gives herself both in this book and in her earlier one—indolence, disorder, gluttony, and, given a sensuality focused on oral sex, lesbianism—are the characteristics used in nineteenth-century literature (fictional as well as sociological) to stereotype prostitutes.[11] And given the fact that at the turn of the century artist's models occupied a peculiar place in the social field that was partly that of the *"insoumise"* (the woman exchanging sex for money who is not registered with the police), this stereotype is not irrelevant to Fernande's need to project herself simultaneously as a kind of sex goddess and neophyte.[12] In short we encounter that strange hallucinatory space of the dime novel, the *roman-feuilleton*, the "Harlequin romance": a story of redemption draped over a core of soft porn.

If this is a recipe lifted from the world of daydream and catapulted into cheap literature in order to titillate its readers, Mailer has proved one of its avid consumers. To be sure, he has his suspicions of this text: "Questions do arise. We are dealing with a manuscript that was composed when she was in her seventies. . . . While *Souvenirs Intimes* is written more or less artlessly, the effect is not unprofessional, narrative skills are certainly present, and there is an elevated hint of the romance novel—indeed, it is an elegant example of the form. One has to wonder how much of this book Fernande Olivier wrote herself" (147). Nevertheless, Mailer devotes page after page to its transcription, including an endless scene of cunnilingus (121–23) carried out on the semiconsciously willing

Fernande by both a man and a woman (this takes place before she leaves her hapless marriage and comes to Paris to live under the protection of a sculptor whom she supports by modeling and with whom she moves to the Bateau-Lavoir in the third year of their relationship). And while he is endlessly skeptical about the accounts of themselves given elsewhere by such characters as Guillaume Apollinaire and Gertrude Stein, Mailer accepts pretty much the whole of Fernande's story as it concerns both her sexuality—"her journey from disgust and frigidity into concupiscence" (148)—and her claims to a literary and artistic culture that enabled her to render the dramatis personae of her milieu with great sharpness and insight— "the personages in this second book are evaluated with enough composure to suggest that she has absorbed a few lessons from Flaubert" (99).

Because, for example, Fernande has nothing whatever to say about Max Jacob as a *poet* and can only depict him as tremendously funny doing his outrageous skits and singing his dirty songs—indeed, the only verse she sees fit to transcribe is an example of the latter—this persistent claim to a literary culture is symptomatically interesting. For it would seem to tie the knot between the fact that the story of her life reads like a dime novel and the fact that according to her own account this was the diet she consumed as an adolescent. In the third entry of the diary that she claims she began on her fifteenth birthday, she confesses to the great consolation she got from reading and how, forbidden access to this material by her caricaturally nasty aunt, she was provided by her uncle with "books that would initiate me into life." The very first of these she goes on to list is Eugène Sue's *Les mystères de Paris*, the *roman-feuilleton* of all time (17).

If Fernande's story poses the question of how a strictly brought-up petit-bourgeois girl runs away to Paris to become a career bohemienne—that is, something of a semiprostitute—the answer seems to lie in a kind of romance reading that opened up the space of artistic production for her as both imaginatively exciting and singularly redemptive—culture having the power to sublimate moral laxity and to raise up those in the lowest depths to the highest honor.[13] A product of "Bovaryism," she is shaped by her reading and, imitating the plots of the novels that thrilled her, she produces "herself" as yet one more version of their story. It is for this reason that her narrative sounds like theirs, not only in its outline but in the texture of its prose. Just as it is for this reason we feel, inside it, as though we were in a hall of mirrors, not knowing whether a detail of her life sounds like an event in a dime novel because it happened in imitation of one or because, never having happened, it is being retrojected onto the flow of past time on the basis of one.

The term "Bovaryism" should, of course, place Fernande within a context that is much richer, sociologically and artistically, than Picasso studies and the problem of how to take seriously an eyewitness account by someone who lived through the long battle of the creation of the *Demoiselles d'Avignon* but doesn't seem to have noticed.[14] Bovaryism reminds us of the conviction, older than modernism itself, that it is not art that imitates life but quite the reverse.

The application of this lesson to the very life of the artist came most emphatically at the hands of the Russian formalists who began to address this problem in the late 1920s. Perhaps its most colorful version was advanced by Roman Jakobson, quoting Mayakovsky, "who wrote that even a poet's style of dress, even his intimate conversations with his wife should be determined by the whole of his poetic production. He understood very well the close connection between poetry and life."[15] But certainly it was given its most historically reasoned exposition in Boris Tomashevsky's "Literature and Biography," where the "biographical artist" is explained as an invention of the romantic period, never having existed before that (Tomashevsky reminds us of the biographyless Shakespeare, whom he calls "the 'iron mask' of literature").[16] But far from being a distraction from the work itself—which in the eyes of a formalist would indeed be a fault—this invention, producing something we could call the author function, enters as one more element in the creative matrix that *is* the "work itself." To dramatize the way these biographies are themselves poetic or artistic constructions, Tomashevsky turns to Byron as his classic example. "Byron, the poet of sharp-tempered characters, created the canonical biography for a lyrical poet," he says. For the formalists, then, it was out of the question that one lived one's biography; rather, as an artist, one created it, so that it was one's art that produced the pattern of one's life.

That such a reversal might be true of Picasso has recently been admitted by William Rubin. This position comes in the midst of the almost frenzied biography industry that has been in operation since the 1950s, which is based on the conviction that so slavishly does Picasso's art follow his real-life adventures that, "if there were no lacunae in our biographic data about Picasso, there would be no lacunae in our interpretations of his art."[17] Referring to Sabartès's claim that "with each new amorous experience, we see [Picasso's] art progress, new forms, another language, a particular expression to which one could give the name of a woman," Rubin objects as follows: "That Picasso's homes and friends should alter with serious new loves is hardly surprising. But Picasso's artistic language was clearly *not* determined by the entries and exits of different lovers. On the contrary, it might well be argued that these entries and exits were themselves determined by Picasso's desire to explore differing realms of artistic and emotional experience."[18]

One such example might come from 1926, when Picasso is understood by many scholars as indeed having had a desire for new artistic frontiers. Since this is the moment when surrealism appeared on the horizon of his experience, beckoning not only with an elaborate campaign of adulation but with the dramatic evidence that its own stable of artists—most impressively in the example of fellow Spaniard Joan Miró—was capable of producing painting that was both new and inspired. For an artist whose work had become as lax and routinized as Picasso's had by 1924–25, when neoclassicism could certainly have no longer seemed a viable course to follow, the ideas promulgated by André Breton of an art produced unconsciously might well have been seductive. And indeed it was in 1926 that Picasso executed two collages—rendered in a fetishlike combination of cloth and nails and dedicated to the revelation of personal pain—that many observers have felt were somehow in the debt of psychic automatism, for their emotional tone even if not directly for their formal inspiration.

But psychic automatism had certain formal features as well, particularly in the hands of Miró, who deployed it in the creation of a linear meander that exchanged the cubist grid for an organicist labyrinth to generate such major paintings as *The Harlequin's Carnival*. It is just such a weblike meander that structures what is Picasso's only large-scale effort of 1926, a painting done in the first months of the year and called *The Milliner's Workshop* (Fig. 71). That the painting is not only formally but operationally in surrealism's orbit was attested to by Picasso in a statement he made just one year later, at the time of Juan Gris's death in May of 1927. "I had made a large black, gray, and white painting," he said. "I didn't know what it represented, but I saw Gris on his deathbed, and it was my picture."[19] This idea of a work being precipitated from the unconscious—"I didn't know what it represented"—is helped along, of course, by the nocturnal and thus dreamlike effect of the work's black, white, and gray tonalities but also by the apparent attempt to give way to the unconscious impulses of the hand in forming its compositional network.

And, as in the case of dream analysis, Picasso went on in

the month or so after having made the painting, to elaborate separate details from within it in a sequence of drawings committed to a sketchbook dated March 21–June 20, 1926. In these drawings, mostly devoted to heads and torsos of the little shop girls from the big canvas, two features emerge despite the large stylistic range of the sketches (Figs. 74, and 75). First there is the conflation of profile and front face to produce a duality within the single head (a redoubling that occurs whether Picasso is following the laws of synthetic cubism or proceeding by means of an "automatist," curvilinear tracery). Second there is the repetition of certain facial characteristics: a wide oval face, a Roman nose bridging straight from the forehead, and short-cropped blond hair. These are the features that—rehearsed again and again in these pages and, according to a certain logic, released by the automatism of his own desire—would enter Picasso's actual life just one year later in the person of Marie-Thérèse Walter (Fig. 72).

Seeing her leaving the Galeries Lafayette just as he was emerging from the subway, he rushed up to her and said, "Mademoiselle, you have an interesting face. I would like to paint your portrait. I am Picasso." According to both Marie-Thérèse and Picasso, this happened in January of 1927, when she was just seventeen.[20] Her age and his marriage meant that they would then embark on a secret liaison that he would encode in his art. As this developed throughout the thirties it took on certain features that would come to be named the "Marie-Thérèse style" and to be thought of as having been called into being by her arrival in his life. But the evidence of

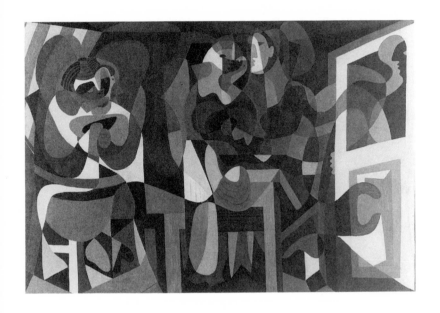

71.
The Milliner's Workshop
January 1926

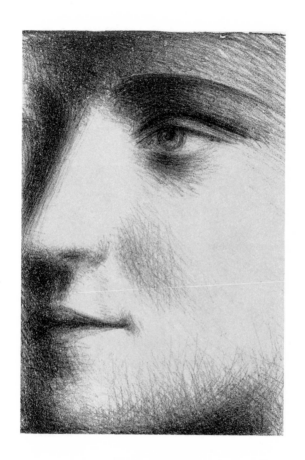

72.
Visage
1928

73.
*Bather Lying
Down*
1920

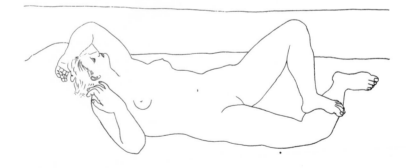

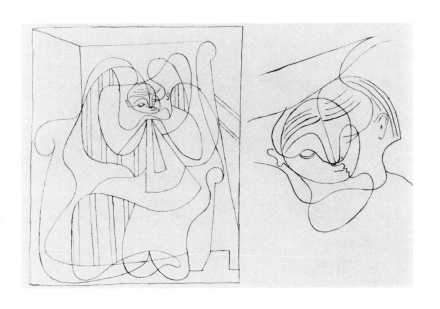

74.
Page from Sketchbook, "Paris, 21 mars, 1926"

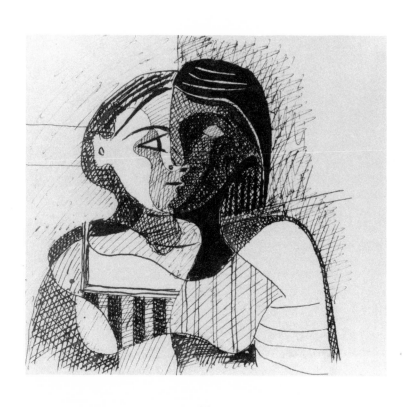

75.
Page from Sketchbook, "Paris, 21 mars, 1926"

the 1926 sketchbook and its possibly unconscious fantasy of both a sexual object and a stylistic web within which to set it would suggest the opposite: that Picasso, having invented this turn in his art, went out—*amour fou*–style—and found it. The casting director of his own script, he pounced on this Grecian look-alike who happened to be called Marie-Thérèse.[21]

The biography industry is relentless, however, indefatigable. So an amateur Picasso sleuth has taken exactly the same evidence for seeing Marie-Thérèse as having literally been called into existence by the demands of Picasso's art to argue just the opposite: that if a young blond appears in the 1926 sketchbook and the large painting to which it relates, this can only be because Picasso already knew her in real life.[22] Further, since this type appears in Picasso's work not just in 1926 but also as early as 1925, the argument is that Picasso must have begun his connection to Marie-Thérèse two years before the date claimed by all the parties concerned, the famous scene of their meeting having occurred not when she was seventeen but when she was fifteen. To all the possible objections— Why would Picasso have told Françoise Gilot a lie on this subject? Why would he have misidentified the subject of *The Milliner's Workshop* when it was exhibited in the 1950s, long after Marie-Thérèse had become public knowledge and there was no reason to pretend that this was a shop across the street from him on the rue de la Boétie, if in fact it was Marie-Thérèse's house in the suburbs?—the answer turns on Picasso's fanatical interest in secrecy and his delight in mystifying scholars.[23] But there are still major problems with this account.

One is a near infinite regress of "Marie-Thérèse images" before the proposed 1925 encounter, one of which is clearly dated on its front "1924" (which would now have Picasso meeting her when she was fourteen), and this one is so disturbing to this account that its author claims that the picture was actually finished early in 1925.[24] Another belongs in the dime novel department, since the scenario being projected here has Picasso courting the fifteen-year-old Marie-Thérèse, Humbert Humbert style, by taking her to the circus and the movies, plying her with ice cream cones, and paying long visits to her mother in their suburban villa for a year and a half before he was able to begin a sexual relation with her.[25] If scholars would rather believe that their hero could take a role in *Lolita* than consider that his escape from his emotional and aesthetic cul-de-sac was being plotted in his art in the mid-1920s, this is of course their prerogative.[26]

But the structuralist considerations about biography elaborated by the Russian formalists would call our attention to yet another feature of the image bank in question. This is the onset, beginning in 1924, of the double face, formed by a composite of frontal view and superimposed profile. The "Marie-Thérèse style" explanation wants to make this a feature of Picasso's relation to his model and thus a "proof" that such a connection must coincide with the appearance of this phenomenon in his work. The structuralists, however, would link this feature to the "device." And their explanation would follow the pattern of Jakobson's discussion of *byt* in his extraordinary essay "On a Generation That Squandered Its Poets," in which he treats Mayakovsky's suicide.

Mayakovsky's suicide is an important test case for formalist theory, since common sense would tie it causally to real-world events, most obviously to the poet's increasingly troubled relation to the Russian Revolution. And indeed it is common sense that Jakobson hears from all sides in 1930 on this subject, in expressions of shock at this symptom of a sudden breakdown in the relationship between Mayakovsky and the heroic theme of his work. There is universal agreement over the unexpectedness of this occurrence and insistence on its incompatibility with "the Mayakovsky we knew." *Pravda* summarizes this conviction by announcing, "His death is just as inconsistent with the life he led as it is unmotivated by his poetry."[27]

Motivation is of course an arresting word here because it is precisely the one—although turned absolutely inside out—that the formalists summoned to describe the relation of "event" to form. Understanding the goal of the work of art as a type of perceptual renewal, a revivification of experience, the formalists saw the aesthetic "device" (the specific formal operations) as the work's structural lever on the expectations of its receiver. Therefore insofar as aesthetic experience is a function of the "device," everything else in the artistic object can be seen as so many forms of staging that formal maneuver. Does a character go on a journey? Does the heroine fall ill? These events do not constitute the point of the narrative so much as they serve as the alibi of its form. Having for their function the "motivation" of the device, they then "cause" or call for the text's *real* occasion: the serial retardations, the roughened textures, the effects of estrangement that are its actual goal, the deepest sources of its pleasure. And what is true of a story's turn of plot is equally true of the artist's real-life events. Those, as well, are produced for the sake of his art; they, like everything else with semantic content, are there to "motivate the device."

Now, far from being unheralded by anything in "the Mayakovsky we knew," suicide, Jakobson points out, was an enduring theme of the poet's work. Indeed, "Mayakovsky's most intense poems, 'Man' (1916) and 'About That' (1923), are dedicated to it."[28] Yet if this theme was gripping for the poet—and this is Jakobson's real, formalist point—it was because it was a semantic marker for one of the major poles of the structural opposition that functioned as the dynamic of his art. This opposition is between stasis and motion, between a deadening immobility and a victory over that sameness, in a movement that will overtake, outstrip, transcend time. The figure that is the controlling trope of Mayakovsky's art, sending him racing after the invention of new rhythms, is thus the very figure of the dialectic, and it is this rather than politics that, Jakobson claims, married Mayakovsky to the revolution. October, Jakobson argues, was simply one more trope for the Mayakovskian system: "Weariness with fixed and narrow confines, the urge to transcend static boundaries—such is

Mayakovsky's infinitely varied theme." The revolution, in this sense, merely motivates the device.

The term Jakobson uses for this hated narrowness and fixity refers to the form it takes in many of the poet's verses, in which the Russian word *byt* repeatedly surfaces. Literally meaning "quotidian" or "everyday," *byt* functioned for Mayakovsky in something of the same way that spleen operated for Baudelaire. It seemed to him an immutable present, something inertial, stagnating, stifling. "It is the poet's primordial enemy," Jakobson tells us, "and he never tired of returning to this theme. 'Motionless *byt*.' . . . 'Slits of *byt* are filled with fat and coagulate, quiet and wide.' "[29] *Byt* was Mayakovsky's enemy, the personification of an entropic stoppage of time, the equivalent of poetic failure, the figure of rhythmic implosion, of stale, fetid verse. As, from his earliest work, he thought of its possible triumph, he wrote, "Mama! / Tell my sisters, Ljuda and Olja, / That there's no way out." And from this earliest scenario forward, the theme—structural, symbolic— advances. What followed, for Jakobson was that

gradually the idea that "there's no way out" lost its purely literary character. From the poetic passage it found its way into prose, and "there's no way out" turned up as an author's remark in the margin of the manuscript for "About That." And from that prose context the same idea made its way into the poet's life: in his suicide note he said: "Mama, sisters, comrades, forgive me. This is not a good method (I don't recommend it to others), but for me there's no other way out."[30]

The idea of suicide had long motivated the device of temporal dynamism for Mayakovsky. Eventually it became the only way to "write" paralysis.

And for Picasso? The amateur scholar who wants Picasso to have met Marie-Thérèse in 1925 reads the double head as the superimposition of Picasso's profile on his mistress's face, the male shadow cast onto the female receptacle as a thematic exploration of the anticipated and then enacted sexual relation. Any reasonable assessment of these double physiognomies, however, emerging as they both do from feminine bodies, would read them as two contrasted females, one light and one dark—would see them function, that is, as an oppositional pair.

That Picasso thought of women through the matrix of the oppositional pair is remarked by Françoise Gilot as she remembers Picasso's attraction to the sight of her sitting with one of her friends in a restaurant:

I must admit I wondered more than once whether, if he had met me alone, he would even have noticed me. Meeting me with Geneviève, he saw a theme that runs throughout his entire work and was particularly marked during the 1930s: two women together, one fair and the other dark, the one all curves and the other externalizing

her internal conflicts, with a personality that goes beyond the pictorial; one, the kind of woman who has a
purely aesthetic and plastic life with him, the other, the
type whose nature is reflected in dramatic expression.
When he saw the two of us that morning, he saw in
Geneviève a version of formal perfection, and in me,
who lacked that formal perfection, a quality of unquiet
which was actually an echo of his own nature. That
created an image for him, I'm sure. He even said, "I'm
meeting beings I painted twenty years ago." It was certainly one of the original causes of the interest he
showed.[31]

That there was a feminine type to which he was drawn
was something Picasso announced to her early in their relationship—"You know, I've always been haunted by a certain
few faces and yours is one of them"—and that these types
came in pairs was something she was able to plot for herself.
But while Gilot speaks of this as a "theme," the Russian formalists would see it differently. It is, they would say, the constructed "event" used to motivate the "device." And in
Picasso's case the device is the structural control of the oppositional pair itself, whether precipitated spatially, through
the radical disconnection between vertical and horizontal
axes—visual and tactile spaces, as in the *Still Life with Chair
Caning*[32]—or produced as the semiological opposition of the
"paradigm" that promotes the circulation of the sign; or

whether, far more narratively, it is spun out as the juxtaposition of two female types, the overt and the covert, the dark and the fair, the elegant and the voluptuous.

This book has been about the structuralist paradigm and the degree to which Picasso controlled it in the opening years of the teens. But it has also been about the way the paradigm eventually came to control *him*, at the point when the oppositional structure begins to work on an entirely different pattern and, as John Berger reminds us, history begins to fail Picasso. This second structure I have modelled on reaction formation, in which the presumed opposition constructs events according to an insidious logic, so that what is forbidden is allowed to continue, although transposed, in the very features of what is permitted.

Reaction formation as a structure was, I have argued, the motor operating Picasso's commitment to pastiche; but it is also, finally, the hook that addicts him to secrecy, to the elaboration of a fanatically hidden life that is nonetheless extensively coded onto the entirely public surfaces of his painting, in just the style of the obsessional whose ritualized behavior performs—in the modality of cleanliness—the very libidinally charged compulsions he has "successfully" repressed.

But even further, secrecy itself has implications with regard to the subject who practices it. For, by implying the importance, even the *existence*, of what is hidden, secrecy also seems to underwrite the autonomy of the subject who constructs his or her persona around this response to and protection of a treasured object. Yet if such a subject is caught up within the logical loop of a secret that is projected rather than found (or found *because* projected), then the treasury is empty and the story, told over and over again, is a fantasy, patterned on the tales of others, that the subject undertakes to live.

Thus Mailer is right about the bond between Fernande and Picasso: that its romance produces life itself shaped as the stuff of novels. But this fictitious condition only begins to shape her account long after he's left her and when she's been replaced by another voluptuous innocent; and it transpires not on the level of the existential novel but rather according to the structure of Bovaryism and the *roman-feuilleton*, which is to say, as imitation and stereotype.

The "dime novel" is not, however, what is most central to this cautionary tale. Rather, it is the historical logic of modernism itself, in which the newly liberated circulation of the token-sign always carries as its potential reverse an utterly devalued and empty currency. Pastiche is not necessarily the destiny of modernism, but it is its guilty conscience.

NOTES

INTRODUCTION: A PENNY FOR PICASSO

1. Félix Fénéon, *Oeuvres* (Paris: Gallimard, 1948), 335.

2. Cited in Joan Ungersma Halperin, *Félix Fénéon: Aesthete and Anarchist in Fin-de-Siècle Paris* (New Haven: Yale University Press, 1988), 358.

3. Fénéon, *Oeuvres*, 33.

4. Ibid., 32.

5. André Gide, "Journal of *The Counterfeiters*," appended to *The Counterfeiters*, trans. Dorothy Bussy (New York: Modern Library, 1951), 410. Further citations appear in the text.

6. The specific treatment of *The Counterfeiters* is in Jean-Joseph Goux, *The Coiners of Language* (1984), trans. Jennifer Curtiss Gage (Norman: University of Oklahoma Press, 1994). Goux's other developments of the general theory are in *Symbolic Economies: After Marx and Freud*, trans. Jennifer Curtiss Gage (Ithaca: Cornell University Press, 1990); *Economie et symbolique* (Paris: Seuil, 1973); and *Les iconoclastes* (Paris: Seuil, 1978).

7. Both articles are cited in Michel Sanouillet, *Dada à Paris* (Paris: J. J. Pauvert, 1965), 120, 201.

8. Ibid., 200.

9. Ibid., 62.

10. See ch. 2.

11. Theodor W. Adorno, *Philosophy of Modern Music*, trans. Anne G. Mitchell and Wesley V. Blomster (New York: Seabury Press, 1980). Further citations appear in the text.

12. Ferdinand de Saussure, *Course in General Linguistics*, trans. Wade Baskin (New York: McGraw-Hill, 1966), 119. Saussure adds, "In language there are only differences. Even more important: a difference

generally implies positive terms between which the difference is set up; but in language there are only differences *without positive terms*" (120).

13. Although various scholars have discussed cubism and collage in relation to notions of the "sign" (see ch. 1, n. 4), the analysis of this material in terms of the structural-linguistic concept of a purely oppositional system of "differences *without positive terms*" has been conducted by Yve-Alain Bois in "Kahnweiler's Lesson," *Painting as Model* (Cambridge: MIT Press, 1990), and "The Semiology of Cubism," *Picasso and Braque: A Symposium*, ed. Lynn Zelevansky (New York: Museum of Modern Art, 1992), and by me in "Re-Presenting Picasso," *Art in America*, December 1980; "In the Name of Picasso," *The Originality of the Avant-Garde* (Cambridge: MIT Press, 1985); and "The Motivation of the Sign," *Picasso and Braque: A Symposium*.

14. Daniel-Henry Kahnweiler, "Talking to Picasso" (1948), in *A Picasso Anthology: Documents, Criticism, Reminiscences*, ed. Marilyn McCully (London: Arts Council of Great Britain and Thames and Hudson, 1981), 239 (also cited by Yve-Alain Bois in "The Semiology of Cubism").

15. Goux, *The Coiners of Language*, 129.

THE CIRCULATION OF THE SIGN

1. I have used the translation from the lengthy discussion of this collage by Patricia Leighten in her *Re-Ordering the Universe: Picasso and Anarchism, 1897–1914* (Princeton: Princeton University Press, 1989), 126ff.

2. The clipping is from *Bottle and Wineglass* (Autumn–Winter 1912), in Pierre Daix and Joan Rosselet, *Picasso: The Cubist Years 1907–1916*, trans. Dorothy S. Blair (Boston: New York Graphic Society, 1979), catalog number 549; hereafter cited as Daix.

3. The semiological analysis of this collage was first sketched in my "Motivation of the Sign," in *Picasso and Braque: A Symposium*.

4. The earliest literature to speak of the relationship between cubism and the structural linguistics of Ferdinand de Saussure was Pierre Dufour's "Actualité de cubisme," *Critique*, nos. 267–68 (August 1969), 809–25; Jean Laude's "Picasso et Braque, 1910–1914: La transformation des signes," in *Le cubisme: Travaux IV* (Université de Saint-Etienne: CIEREC, 1971); and Daix, in Daix and Rosselet, *Pi-*

casso: The Cubist Years. None of this literature either theorized this relationship or produced detailed analyses of how it might function. Subsequent work on cubism and collage that has done so is my "Re-Presenting Picasso" (1980), 90–96, and "In the Name of Picasso" (1981), in *The Originality of the Avant-Garde and Other Modernist Myths* (Cambridge: MIT Press, 1985), 23–40; Yve-Alain Bois's "Kahnweiler's Lesson" (1987); and Bois's "Semiology of Cubism" and my "Motivation of the Sign," both delivered at the Museum of Modern Art in November 1989 and published in *Picasso and Braque: A Symposium*, 169–208 and 261–86.

The use of "motivation" in the title of my essay plays the psychological sense of the term against the linguistic one. For the linguist, a sign is motivated when it has a demonstrable relation to its referent, either being physically caused by it (as in the case of the "index," in examples such as footprints or medical symptoms) or resemblant to it (as in the case of the "icon," in examples such as portraits or maps or birdcalls). Linguistic signs are categorized as "symbols" and are seen as arbitrary, which is to say unmotivated. The exceptions to this would come in the form of onomatopoeic words (*beep, meow*), in which some amount of resemblance is at work, or in the case of syncategoremes, which are words—like *here, now, today*—that mark the situation of their utterance and are therefore indexical.

5. In her discussion of Picasso's choice of *Le Journal* as his primary source for these collages, Patricia Leighten argues that this mass-circulation republican daily (publishing a million copies of each issue) "was the ideal vehicle for importing into the café settings of the collages the widely publicized war news, descriptive 'walks on the battle field,' and those macabre 'human-interest' stories of murder, suicide, and vandalism that make up another quarter of the newsprint items used in 1912–1914. Picasso never employed anarchist or radical newspapers, which would have replaced description with polemic" (*Re-Ordering the Universe*, 130).

6. Jérome Tharaud, "La guerre des Balkans: La bravoure monténégrine," *Les Soirées de Paris*, no. 10 (1912), 289–92. *Bottle and Wineglass* (Autumn-Winter 1912), Daix 544, employs a cutting describing the Mirdites of Albania, injecting much the same flavor as Tharaud's report does.

7. André Tudesq, "La guerre des Balkans: Tandis que sonne le canon, sur la Bojana . . . ," *Les Soirées de Paris*, no. 11 (1912), 338–44. In

addition to being the managing editor of *Les Soirées de Paris* in 1912, Tudesq was a reporter for *Paris-Midi*, which had sent him to the Balkans as a correspondent.

8. David Cottington's "What the Papers Say: Politics and Ideology in Picasso's Collages of 1912" (*Art Journal*, 47 [Winter 1988], 350–59) acknowledges Leighten's argument (which I summarize on pp. 39, 41–43) that Picasso's selection and placement of the news clippings in these works is not accidental. But taking issue with her claim that they provide us with a view of Picasso's antimilitarist politics, he goes on to say, "What can not be deduced from these facts alone, however, is the *nature* of his interest in such dispatches and their identifiable subject." Asking *how* these cuttings might signify in each work as a whole, and how they might have done so for Picasso in 1912, he concludes that the news of the outside world is imported into these intimate settings via the clippings only to be distanced into a remote background for the experience of the personal: "Radically innovative though these *papiers collés* were, they were yet in ideological terms representations of an aestheticist individualism that underpinned conventional . . . attitudes to the relations between fine art and a wider visual culture" (358). This argument is expanded in his "Cubism, Aestheticism, Modernism" (*Picasso and Braque: A Symposium*), where he insists on Picasso's brand of protest against bourgeois culture as a form of aestheticism, calls the idea of making Picasso's collage practice into the project of a critique of capitalist culture "wishful thinking," and argues that what is represented in the *Suze* collage is precisely "the *dislocation* between the artistic and political avant-gardes" (68, 70).

9. The first to call attention to the punning reference to Mallarmé's "Un coup de dés" was Robert Rosenblum's "Picasso and the Typography of Cubism," reprinted in *Picasso in Retrospect*, ed. Roland Penrose and John Golding (New York: Harper and Row, 1980). In researching Picasso's possible knowledge of this poem, which, though it had been published in *Cosmopolis* in May 1887, was not republished in the Gallimard typographic version until 1914, Christine Poggi not only notes the importance of Mallarmé to, and the fame of this poem within, the Closerie des Lilas circle of poets frequented by Picasso but argues that Albert Thibaudet's 1912 book *La poésie de Stéphane Mallarmé* contained a chapter on "Un coup de dés" that reproduced the first page of the *Cosmopolis* version as well as several other fragments (see Christine Poggi, *In Defiance of Painting: Cubism, Futurism, and the In-*

vention of Collage [New Haven: Yale University Press, 1992], 278).
Cottington, in arguing against Leighten's assumptions that the anarcho-
symbolist movement of the late nineteenth century, which brought
together workers and intellectuals, was still in place in the early twentieth and can be assumed to be Picasso's political framework, speaks of
the withdrawal of intellectuals into an aestheticist context for which
the neosymbolist movement played an important role. Mallarmé, once
more the center of literary debate, was vigorously defended by Gide
in the *NRF* against charges of elitism (Cottington, 352). In "Cubism,
Aestheticism, Modernism," Cottington develops more evidence of this
mallarméisme, referring to contemporary testimony in the writings of
Roger Allard and Ardengo Soffici (66). See also my "Motivation of
the Sign," 274–82.

10. Leighten, *Re-Ordering the Universe*, 127.

11. Ibid., 130, 128.

12. Ibid., 141.

13. In one of the discussions during the Museum of Modern Art symposium held in conjunction with the Picasso/Braque exhibition, Leo
Steinberg argued that, although the small print of the newspaper was
not intended to be read but only to function as "texture, a kind of
precise energy within the field," the larger headlines could be understood as commenting on the formal play of the work itself, one example of which would be found in the *Bottle of Suze*, where the
subhead LA DISLOCATION is "situated opposite the joint of the glass
where the stem and the circle meet," thus naming the work's visual
effect of "dislocation." He concluded that "the body of the text isn't
meant to be read because, as reading matter, it doesn't function pic-
torially; the scale is wrong" *Picasso and Braque: A Symposium*, 78. Leighten's position is that Picasso expected his immediate circle "to read, as
well as to contemplate his collages" (*Re-Ordering the Universe*, 130);
Cottington's view is that at least Picasso read the material and cut it
out according to what he wanted included but that the visual point of
the collages is to make a break between the public and the personal,
distancing the former. He concludes from this that, in the context of
Picasso's work, "the contents of the newspaper cuttings are secondary;
what is primary is the substitution of ready-made surfaces and references to objects for painted and drawn ones—and the possibilities this
substitution contains for spatial ambiguity and contradiction. . . . Before we decipher the objects—and thus beyond them the ambience

and the 'background of events'—we are made aware of how all this is *contingent* on the illusionism and sleight of hand that Picasso has deployed" ("What the Papers Say," 355).

14. Although Leighten insists that Picasso's wider circle would have been intended by him to read the collages (*Re-Ordering the Universe*, 133–34), she presents evidence for arguing that Juan Gris and Blaise Cendrars produce "parallel works" that constitute the "most telling response to the political aspect of Picasso's collages" (132) and that Gris and Braque both take up, although in a much more limited way, Picasso's use of news clippings to punning and ironic effect (141). Poggi also comments on Gris's and Braque's puns in their collages (*In Defiance of Painting*, 158).

15. Leighten, *Re-Ordering the Universe*, 124, 126–27. Leighten expands her earlier discussion of the *Bottle of Suze* collage into an argument about the newspapers and Picasso's practice of "counter-discourse" in "Cubist Anachronisms: Ahistoricity, Cryptoformalism, and Business-as-Usual in New York," *Oxford Art Journal*, 17 (1994), 96–99.

16. Richard Terdiman, *Discourse/Counter-Discourse: The Theory and Practice of Symbolic Resistance in Nineteenth-Century France* (Ithaca: Cornell University Press, 1985), 127; cited in Leighten, "Cubist Anachronisms," 97.

17. Leighten, "Cubist Anachronisms," 99.

18. Mikhail Bakhtin, *Problems of Dostoevsky's Poetics*, trans. Caryl Emerson (Minneapolis: University of Minnesota Press, 1984), 6; further citations are in the text.

19. Roger Shattuck, *The Banquet Years: The Origins of the Avant-Garde in France, 1885 to World War I* (New York: Doubleday, 1961), 263.

20. In my "Re-Presenting Picasso," I analyze this work not only in terms of the linguistic oppositional pair, or paradigm, but in relation to the oppositional pairs through which early art history tried to map a structure of visual meaning, as in Wolfflin's *Principles of Art History*, with its linear vs. painterly, closed vs. open, planar vs. recession, multiple unity vs. organic unity, and clarity vs. unclarity.

21. The poem was written for the catalog for Delaunay's show in Berlin in January 1913, where the painter's series of *Fenêtres* was exhibited. In the December issue of *Der Sturm* Apollinaire published "Reality, Pure Painting," in which he developed Delaunay's ideas about "simultaneism," a concept he adopted for his own poetry.

22. Although this collage has consistently been understood to be ex-

ecuted on a wallpaper ground onto which have been pasted the various elements, consisting of newspaper fragments plus the "Au Bon Marché" label, it was Yve-Alain Bois and Benjamin Buchloh who called my attention to the fact that the entire ground, *including the label*, is a readymade, since the collage is executed on a Bon Marché cardboard box top consisting of decorative paper and parallelepiped label.

23. See Poggi's discussion of the formal problem of the hole within the context of theories of the decorative (*In Defiance of Painting*, 152).

24. See Sima Godfrey, "Haute Couture and Haute Culture," in *A New History of French Literature*, ed. Denis Hollier (Cambridge: Harvard University Press, 1989), 761–69.

25. "Autobiographie," in *Oeuvres complètes*, 663. I am using Godfrey's translation in "Haute Couture," 762.

26. This is on the verso of the clipping from which the "Tchataldja" report is taken for *Violin* (Fig. 1).

27. Fernande Olivier, *Souvenirs intimes: Ecrits pour Picasso* (Paris: Cahlmann-Lévy, 1988), 69. Never divorced from Paul Percheron, to whom she had been married at sixteen, Fernande was going by the name of Debienne or de la Baume (adopted from her next lover, Laurent Debienne) when she met Picasso.

28. Ibid., 39.

29. Xavier de Montepin, *La porteuse de pain*, 1884; *Mémoires de Mogador*, 5 vols. (Paris, Locard-Davi, 1854).

30. Gertrude Stein, *The Autobiography of Alice B. Toklas* (1933) (New York: Vintage, 1961), 111.

31. Sabartès says: "Because he needed to change his life, because he was tired of the circus and cabarets and no longer needed any of that to surmount the boredom of eight years shared with someone else" (*Documents iconographiques* [Geneva: Pierre Cailler, 1954], 314).

32. Octave Uzanne, *Etudes de sociologie féminine: Parisiennes de ce temps* (Paris: Mercure de France, 1910), 39.

33. "Elle se glisse en announce, à la 4ème page des journaux, où elle sait prendre tous les euphémismes du massage, de l'épilation, de la teinture" (Ibid., 406); for an account of women using the *petit annonce* (classified ads) to make amorous contacts, see 415ff.

34. The idea of introducing the work of Georg Simmel into the context of my argument was generously suggested by Michel Feher, who is himself working on a theorization of coquetry. Feher's suggestions came up during an extremely helpful conversation about the structural

problem of relating the semiotic circularity of the sign to the condition of the *fait-divers* as the journalistic equivalent of rumor.

35. Georg Simmel, "Sociability" (1910), in *On Individuality and Social Forms*, ed. Donald N. Levine (Chicago: Chicago University Press, 1971), 135; further citations appear in the text.

36. The word *ascetic* is Robert Rosenblum's, in "Picasso and the Typography of Cubism," 40.

37. Daix, 293; Rosenblum, "Typography of Cubism," 40.

38. Edward Fry, "Picasso, Cubism and Reflexivity," *Art Journal*, 47 (Winter 1988), 301. Fry continues: "The full pun thus reads 'AU BON MARCHE LUN B TROU ICI,' which may be translated as 'One may make a hole here inexpensively.' " Another such reading, less vulgar but equally silly, "finds" the image of a little "man reading a newspaper" in the rendering of the wineglass in *Bowl with Fruit, Violin, and Wineglass* (Daix 530), a schematized rendering of the glass that had become utterly standardized throughout this run of collages (it begins to shift in early 1913, which is one of the bases for Daix's dating for Picasso's production in these years); see Marjorie Perloff, *The Futurist Moment: Avant-Garde, Avant Guerre, and the Language of Rupture* (Chicago: University of Chicago Press, 1986), 49. Christine Poggi subsequently picks this up and repeats it uncritically (*In Defiance of Painting*, 54).

39. This high/low relationship at the level of materials and cultural spaces was first signaled by Rosenblum in his "Picasso and the Typography of Cubism" but first theorized by Tom Crow, in his discussion of "Modernism and Mass Culture," in *Modernism and Modernity*, ed. Benjamin Buchloh (Halifax: Nova Scotia College of Art Press, 1983), 245–46. The mass-cultural reading has become standard in the subsequent literature on collage. For example, Christine Poggi's development of this position is that Picasso's and Braque's collage practice suggests a "complex and paradoxical relation to mass culture," suggesting simultaneously "a denial of the precious, fine art status of traditional works of art as well as an attempt to subvert the seemingly inevitable process by which art becomes a commodity in the modern world" (*In Defiance of Painting*, 128).

40. Tom Crow writes: "The principle of collage construction itself collapses the distinction between high and low by transforming the totalizing creative practice of traditional painting into a fragmented consumption of already existing manufactured images" (*Modernism and Modernity*, 246). The straight pins used to affix the collage pieces to the

paper surface, so that they could be tested and repositioned, are still prominently affixed to some of the collages (Daix 601 and 603).

41. Gertrude Stein, *Picasso* (1938) (Boston: Beacon Press, 1959), 27.

42. Cottington, "What the Papers Say," 355–57. In his later expansion of this argument, Cottington quotes the contemporary reception of Picasso and Braque to show that at the time their work was perceived as "a kind of *mallarméisme composite*": the critic Roger Allard accused it of being mystificatory and sterile for just this reason, while the painter and poet Ardengo Soffici praised its "elliptical syntax" and "grammatical transpositions," which he compared with Mallarmé's. See Cottington, "Cubism, Aestheticism, Modernism," in *Picasso and Braque: A Symposium*, 66.

43. Cottington, "Cubism, Aestheticism, Modernism," 69.

44. Christine Poggi writes: "Collage works, by bringing [journalism, advertising, and machine-made, cheap simulacra] and other elements of commercial culture within the domain of painting and drawing, function as a critique, not only of prevailing market conditions, but also of the futility of the Symbolist response to these conditions" and "For Picasso [unlike Mallarmé], the effacement of the self did not gesture towards the pure, expressive radiance of words. Rather, the artist's use of newspaper and other mass-produced materials signaled the obsolescence of contemporary cultural hierarchies and theories of representation in an age in which cultural artifacts had become commodities" (*In Defiance of Painting*, 129, 153).

45. Stéphane Mallarmé, "Grands Faits Divers," in *Oeuvres complètes* (Paris: Gallimard-Pléiade, 1945), 398–422.

46. Tailhade's remark was a response to a bomb thrown by the anarchist August Vaillant into the Chamber of Deputies on December 9, 1893. By January 1894, *Le Gaulois* was publishing mug shots of "les anarchistes intellectuels" (taken from the illustrations for *Les hommes d'aujourd'hui*—the series for which Mallarmé had supplied his biographical note). On April 4 of that year, a bomb went off in the fashionable restaurant Foyot, injuring only one person, Laurent Tailhade, who lost an eye. Félix Fénéon stood trial for this action, along with thirty other suspected anarchists. Mallarmé rose to his defense in statements to the press: "M. Fénéon is one of our most distinguished young writers and a remarkable art critic. . . . You say they are talking of detonators. Certainly, for Fénéon, there were no better detonators than his articles" (cited in Joan Ungersma Halperin, *Félix Fénéon*, 282).

47. Robert Greer Cohn, *Mallarmé's* Divagations*: A Guide and Commentary* (New York: Peter Lang, 1990), 335. Further citations of the "Grands Faits Divers" are to this translation and appear in the text.

48. Mallarmé, "Crise de vers," in *Oeuvres complètes*, 368; "Crisis in Poetry," in *Mallarmé: Selected Prose Poems, Essays, and Letters*, trans. Bradford Cook (Baltimore: Johns Hopkins Press, 1956), 42.

49. "Mimique," in *Oeuvres complètes*, 310.

50. "Crayonné au théatre," in *Oeuvres complètes*, 296, as cited in Jacques Derrida, "The Double Session" (1970), in *Dissemination*, trans. Barbara Johnson (Chicago: University of Chicago Press, 1981), 244.

51. Derrida, "Double Session," 262.

52. Ibid., 264.

53. Daix writes: "The headline undoubtedly referred to the war in the Balkans, but he was clearly applying it to the battle in painting" (127). This summarizes the position stated by William Rubin, who suggests that the battle refers to a competition between Picasso and Braque over "the use of the new medium" (*Picasso and Braque: Pioneering Cubism* [New York: Museum of Modern Art, 1989], 28). In *Picasso and Braque: A Symposium*, Jack Flam agrees: "It is a collage combining several different pictorial languages which are contrasted to each other: *la bataille qui s'est engagée* is the war between these various languages" (87).

54. Cottington, "What the Papers Say," 359.

55. Saying: "Possibly it is too late to speak of cubism. The time for experimentation is passed. Our young artists are interested now in creating definitive works." Apollinaire's praise in his lecture for Delaunay, Léger, Duchamp, and Picabia could not have pleased Picasso. See Francis Steegmuller, *Apollinaire: Poet among the Painters* (New York: Farrar, Straus, 1981), 235.

56. Guillaume Apollinaire, *Apollinaire on Art: Essays and Reviews; 1901–1918*, ed. LeRoy C. Breunig (New York: Viking, 1972), 199.

57. Guillaume Apollinaire, "L'antitradition futuriste" (1913), in *Oeuvres complètes de Guillaume Apollinaire*, ed. Michel Décaudin (Paris: André Balland et Jacques Lecat, 1966), 877–79. The manifesto was published in French and Italian, in July 1913, as a broadside, then published in French in *Gil Blas* (August 3, 1913) and in Italian in *Lacerba* (September 15, 1913).

58. Daix, *Picasso: Life and Art*, trans. Olivia Emmet (London: Thames and Hudson, 1994), 114, 404, n. 13. The one exception to Picasso's

declared stand against futurism is his sudden adoption of Ripolin commercial enamels in April 1912. Severini was in Picasso's studio when
Braque came back after having been absent from Paris the entire spring
and, seeing them on a canvas for the first time, exclaimed, "On change
son fusil d'épaule!" ("So, we're changing sides, are we!"—this has
somehow entered the Anglophone literature as "we're changing weap-
ons," which is not what it means in colloquial French. Cited in Gino
Severini, *Tutta la vita di un pittore*, vol. 1 [Rome: Garzanti, 1946], 141).
The "side" Braque might have been referring to was futurism's touting
not only of modern subjects but of modern materials, such as constructions employing electric lightbulbs, etc. (See, e.g., Boccioni's "Technical Manifesto," 1912.) This kind of furtive acknowledgment of the
position of what he perceived as the enemy, even while denying it, is
a function of what I analyze in the next chapter as Picasso's engagement
in a structure of reaction formation. This structure of ambivalence
might explain the puzzling fact that while Picasso introduced oil cloth
printed with a pattern of chair caning in the spring of 1912—another
example of a futurist sense of materials—he developed it no further until
Braque's introduction of wood-grained wallpaper into a drawing, in
September of the same year, produced a wholly different sense of the
possibilities of this procedure, one that was not at all "futurist" in spirit.
59. Speaking of his easel and stand for sculptures, Picasso writes to
Kahnweiler, "If you don't think it's wise to keep them at the boulevard
de Clichy, then I think we should put them in storage" (Daix, *Picasso:
Life and Art*, 117). Daix clarifies that this need for caution was because
of Fernande.
60. Ibid., 115.

Picasso/Pastiche

1. The Swedish artist Arvid Fougstedt published the following description of the rue Schoelcher studio in *Svenska Dagbladt* (January 9,
1916): "The studio is as vast as a church. Four or five hundred canvases
of varying sizes are stacked against the walls, on the table and on the
easels. The floor is scattered with pieces of cut-out paper that he glues
onto his canvases—because Picasso utilizes also newspapers, wrapping
paper, cinema tickets, which he glues on his paintings here or there as
it pleases him. At each step, I trample palettes, empty tubes of paint,
brushes. . . . I consider the studio and am stupefied by the number of

canvases; what imagination, what profusion of ideas! . . . I don't know where to start in this mess. The pictures are arranged like the scales of a fish to take up the least possible space and Picasso circles around ceaselessly to displace and relocate them" (cited in Billy Klüver, *Un jour avec Picasso* [Paris: Hazan, 1994], 47).

2. Cocteau's first meeting with Picasso was dated in the literature, by Pierre Daix and others, as December 1915. It now appears that Cocteau was actually introduced to Picasso by Edgar Varèse in the summer of 1915 (see Billy Klüver and Julie Martin, *Kiki's Paris: Artists and Lovers, 1900–1930* [New York: Abrams, 1989], n. 94).

3. Letter of December 9, 1915, cited in Daix, 348. It is from this letter that we learn that the *Harlequin* left Picasso's studio in early December, having been bought by Léonce Rosenberg.

4. Jean Cocteau, *Picasso* (Paris: Stock, 1923); reprinted in Jean Cocteau, *Entre Picasso et Radiguet* (Paris: Hermann, 1967), 120.

5. The costume is most visible in the portraits of Jacinto Salvado, painted wearing it in 1923; see Christian Zervos, *Pablo Picasso*, V (Paris: Cahiers d'Art, 1952), nos. 17, 23, 37, and 135.

6. Cocteau, *Entre Picasso et Radiguet*, p. 122.

7. *Le Nouveau Spectateur*, October 25, 1919, 28; cited in Kenneth Silver, *Esprit de Corps* (Princeton: Princeton University Press, 1989), 244.

8. Françoise Gilot and Carlton Lake, *Life with Picasso* (New York: McGraw-Hill, 1964), 217.

9. Silver, *Esprit de Corps*, 252.

10. Gérard Genette, *Palimpsestes* (Paris: Seuil, 1982), 144.

11. Pierre Daix, *Picasso: Life and Art*, 162: "Picasso simply and naturally wished to assume the heritage of French painting at its most classic. His ambition was to encompass and become the modern point of convergence of Poussin, Cézanne, and Ingres."

12. Marie-Laure Bernadac, *Bonjour, M. Manet* (Paris: Centre Georges Pompidou, 1983), 45.

13. Wilhelm Uhde, *Picasso et la tradition française* (Paris: 1928), 55–56.

14. See the discussion in Silver, *Esprit de Corps*, 28–56.

15. Cocteau, letter to Valentine Hugo, August 13, 1916; cited in Billy Klüver, "A Day with Picasso," *Art in America*, 74 (September 1986), 103.

16. Ibid., 161. Cocteau didn't write to Valentine Hugo announcing that Picasso had agreed to participate in *Parade* until August 24, 1916.

17. Pierre Daix, "Le retour de Picasso au portrait (1914–1921): Une

problématique de généralization du cubisme," in *Le retour à l'ordre, 1919–1925* (Université de Saint-Etienne: CIEREC, 1975), 81–94. John Richardson also stresses the fragility of Cocteau's supposed hold on Picasso's imagination. After saying that at first "Picasso wanted nothing to do with Cocteau" and adding that "even Diaghilev . . . did not really trust him either as a collaborator or friend," Richardson pictures Picasso's brief amusement at Cocteau's antics before summing up Picasso's opinion at the time of the *Parade* opening: "Picasso agreed with the young poet Pierre Reverdy, who described Cocteau as 'the sandwich man of the period' and asked him why, coming from so far and setting out so late, should he push ahead of everyone else" (*A Life of Picasso: 1907–1917*, vol. 2 [New York: Random House, 1996], 380, 381, 420).

18. Daix, "Le retour de Picasso," 88.

19. Ibid., 90, 92.

20. Douglas Cooper, *Picasso, Theatre* (New York: Abrams, 1987), 31.

21. Daniel-Henry Kahnweiler, "Entretiens avec Picasso," *Quadrum*, no. 2 (November 1956), 74.

22. André Salmon, *Souvenirs sans fin*, vol. 2 (Paris: Gallimard, 1956), 199–200.

23. Pierre Cabanne, *Pablo Picasso, His Life and Times*, trans. Harold J. Salemson (New York: Morrow, 1977), 196.

24. This exchange between Kahnweiler and her was recounted to me by Teri Wehn-Damisch.

25. Gilot, *Life with Picasso*, 359.

26. Pierre Daix, who is otherwise busy producing a buoyant, confident, controlling, masterful Picasso, breaks this rhythm in his book to confide of his subject in 1946: "Picasso would not have been Picasso if this sense of euphoria had driven out every vestige of anxiety" (*Picasso: Life and Art*, 289).

27. Gilot, *Life with Picasso*, 153.

28. Ibid., 156.

29. Ibid., 230.

30. Jaime Sabartés, *Picasso: Documents iconographiques*, no. 118.

31. Brassaï, *Picasso and Company*, trans. Francis Price (New York: Doubleday, 1966), 47.

32. Fernande Olivier, *Picasso et ses amis* (Paris: Stock, 1933), 219–20.

33. Anne Baldassari, *Picasso, Photographe* (Paris: Musée Picasso, 1994), 214–15.

34. Ibid., 16.

35. Ibid., 11, 21.

36. Olivier, *Picasso et ses amis*, 166.

37. Paul Haviland, "We Are Living in the Age of the Machine," *291*, nos. 7–8 (September-October 1915), 1.

38. William Camfield, *Francis Picabia* (Princeton: Princeton University Press, 1979), 82, n. 32.

39. These were *Udnie* and *Edtaonisl.*

40. Daix, in *Picasso and Braque: A Symposium*, 212. Elsewhere Daix says: "For him total abstraction was decorative, the death of art" (*Picasso: Life and Art*, 152).

41. Daix, in *Picasso and Braque: A Symposium*, 212.

42. *Voilà* ELLE is certainly a response to, if not a plagiarism of, Duchamp's *Bride* from the Large Glass. And indeed, if I am addressing Picabia's work in relation to Picasso's reaction to developments in 1915, this is because it was Picabia who was disseminating Duchamp's ideas through the vehicle of *291* at this time.

43. This argument is most highly developed in Buchloh's work on Gerhard Richter, particularly "Gerhard Richter: Painting after the Subject of History" (Ph.D. diss., Graduate Center, City University of New York, 1993). See particularly the argument in ch. 3 on "Deskilling the Nude": "While we know that within the arsenal of desublimatory assaults driving the modernist project, deskilling is only *one*, it is crucial for our discussion here to emphasize the various alliances which *deskilling* formed in the course of its historical evolution: from the association with the industrial object to the link with photographic and scientific vision; or from its mimetic embrace of advertising to a general identification with other mass-cultural practices." Buchloh argues that in Seurat's developed drawing style, photography is first linked with deskilling in order to produce the opposite of the "Neoclassical body of promise and plenitude," as well as the effacement of representational skill.

For strategies to mechanize abstraction in relation to the paradigms of the monochrome canvas and the expressionist gesture, see ch. 8, "Gerhard Richter: Painter of the Neo-Avant-Garde."

44. See the title essay in my *The Originality of the Avant-Garde and Other Modernist Myths* (Cambridge: MIT Press, 1986). For Yve-Alain Bois's stress on the importance of working in series to Picasso's development of cubism and collage, see n. 63 below.

45. Dismissing Picabia's dada works as a mere "rehash" of what Picasso had done in "his *papiers collés* and canvases of 1914, in which already he had reduced a bottle of Bass (ale) to Bas (low)," Daix says Picasso saw Picabia as "a painter without personality, someone, he said, who was always trying to make more of himself because he didn't have the skill to make enough" (*Picasso: Life and Art*, 172).

46. Bernard Geiser, *Picasso, peintre-graveur*, vol. 1 (Berne: Kornfeld, 1990), 117.

47. Around the same time Pierre Reverdy was also denouncing the mechanomorph. In his essay "Sur le cubisme," published in the first issue of his magazine *Nord-Sud* (March 15, 1917), Reverdy attacks Picabia's mechanomorphic works not only for their representation of "the most modern objects" but for their use of a written caption ("titre inscrit") to supplement the otherwise inscrutable image. See Etienne-Alain Hubert, "Pierre Reverdy et le cubisme en mars 1917," *Revue de l'art*, 43 (1979), 65.

48. See Daix's discussion, *Picasso: Art and Life*, 144. Alfred Barr also locates the Max Jacob portrait as primarily within the orbit of Cézanne (see *Picasso: Fifty Years of His Art* [New York: The Museum of Modern Art, 1946], 261).

49. See Molly Nesbit's work on Duchamp's relation to mechanical drawing and its implications for the mass-produced and therefore patented object: "The Language of Industry," in *The Definitively Unfinished Marcel Duchamp*, ed. Thierry de Duve (Cambridge: MIT Press, 1991); "Ready-made Originals," *October*, no. 37 (Summer 1986); and "What Was an Author?" *Yale French Studies*, no. 73 (1987).

50. That cubism once again implied the very position that others would develop but Picasso himself will need to reject is to be found in Picasso's own commitment in 1912 to substituting a written code—the words *ma jolie* or *j'aime Eva*—for the iconic representation of his mistress Eva Gouel. Writing Kahnweiler that "I love her very much and I will write this in my paintings," Picasso acknowledges that portraiture is only an option for him at this time via the substitution of a mass-produced sign ("Ma Jolie" being the title of a popular song) for the visual image of his beloved (letter of June 12, 1912, in Rubin, 395).

51. See the discussion of this work in Poggi, *In Defiance of Painting*, 82–84. David Cottington argues that the duplication within collages such as this one, of the conditions of their own consumption by a

small, wealthy group of collectors and dealers, undercuts the ideologically critical edge such works might have had, making them a celebration of the values of privacy and individuality supported by this elite
("What the Papers Say").

52. See, for example, Daix 666 and Figs. 56 and 57, for the implied
mirror frame; Daix 673 and Fig. 57, for the experience of objects
reflected in a mirror; Daix 691 and Figs. 56 and 58, for an exploration
of the object's transparency.

53. Although this notation is to be found next to the work's reproduction as photo no. 377 in the Kahnweiler photoarchive volumes
(Album VI–VII) on deposit at the Galérie Louise Leiris, it has disap-
peared from all subsequent references to this work.

54. See the entry on *The Fireplace* in *Picasso and Things*, ed. Jean Suth-
erland Boggs (Cleveland: Cleveland Museum of Art, 1992), 176–77.
A work from 1915 is signed "Guitar and Clarinet on a Mantelpiece"
(Daix 812). Two other paintings listed as being made at the rue
Schoelcher show fireplaces with mirrors (Daix 887 and 891). Commenting on the latter, however, Joan Rosselet writes of the mantelpiece: "Was this an imaginary fireplace, bearing no relationship to the
environment, or an indication that 887 and 891 were done after the
move from Rue Schoelcher?" (Daix 356). I have not been able to
document whether the rue Schoelcher apartment actually did or did
not have a fireplace, although for an apartment/atelier of that date and
class not to have had one would have been highly unlikely.

55. Robert Delaunay, *Du cubisme à l'art abstrait*, cited in Herschel
Chipp, *Theories of Modern Art* (Berkeley: University of California Press,
168), 318.

56. Daniel-Henry Kahnweiler, *The Rise of Cubism* (1916), trans.
Henry Aronson (New York: Wittenborn, 1949) 8, 10.

57. This is Kahnweiler's position (Ibid., 19). See Braque's explanations
about the return of local color with collage, in Dora Vallier, "Braque,
la peinture et nous (propos de l'artiste)," *Cahiers d'Art 29*, no. 1 (October 1954), 17.

58. In the symposium held in conjunction with the exhibition *Picasso
and Braque: Pioneering Cubism* at the Museum of Modern Art, it was
suggested that the wallpapers Picasso used were originally far more
vivid and that the brown and ocher tones we now encounter are the
result of fading. To this it was objected that in *Musical Instruments* (1913;
Daix 577) Picasso reduplicated one of the frequently used wallpapers

in oils and that the colors are the same in both painting and collages; and further, that in the Musée Picasso there are fragments of the original wallpapers, which had been kept in portfolios by the artist and not exposed to daylight since the time when Picasso was working with them, and that these demonstrate that the wallpapers in the collages have not faded (*Picasso and Braque: A Symposium*, 125, 164).

59. See the discussion in my "Motivation of the Sign."

60. Hubert Damisch has presented Wittgenstein's description of this type of dilemma in the *Tractatus logio-philosophicus* as follows: "In Wittgenstein's terms, an 'image,' a 'portrait,' can describe, picture, represent, in the mode of the *Abbildung*, any reality whose form it has, for example, spatial or colored form. But as for the form of the representation, of the a-presentation, the image or portrait cannot describe or represent this but only show or display it, which is to say . . . *stage it*, in the way painting deploys and makes play with color, displaying it, exhibiting it, but not describing it, depicting it, or simply *imitating* it" (*The Origin of Perspective*, trans. John Goodman [Cambridge: MIT Press, 1994], 268–69).

61. See, for example, Daix 506, 511, 541, 616.

62. *Picasso and Braque: A Symposium*, 166.

63. In his important essay "The Semiology of Cubism," Yve-Alain Bois stresses Picasso's procedure, beginning with the aftermath of the *Demoiselles d'Avignon*, of working in series, a procedure that allowed him to isolate certain syntactical aspects of the group—first the arrislike triangular network that functions as a protogrid, then the rectilinear grid itself, then the scatter of "sickle" hooks detached from the grid and free-floating as a proto–sign system, and finally the fully semiological concept of the sign in collage.

64. Here I am differing slightly with the position taken by Tom Crow, that all aspects of translation of collage into "painted replications" were a fatal compromise to the conceptual coherence of Picasso's and Braque's originally transgressive enterprise; see Thomas Crow, "Modernism and Mass Culture," *Modernism and Modernity*, 251.

65. See my discussion of this operation in "In the Name of Picasso," *The Originality of the Avant-Garde*, 37–38.

66. Crow's condemnation reads: "After Braque's departure for the war, Picasso retained the identification with mass culture, but now only in the terms which the culture industry itself dictates. . . . The translation of the collage pieces into painted replications folds the noisy,

heterogeneous scene of fringe leisure into the sonority of museum painting" ("Modernism and Mass Culture," 250–51). Greenberg's assessment is more neutral: "Only when the collage had been exhaustively translated into oil, and transformed by this translation, did cubism become an affair of positive color and flat, interlocking silhouettes whose legibility and placement created allusions to, if not the illusion of, unmistakable three-dimensional identities" (Clement Greenberg, "Collage," *Art and Culture* [Boston: Beacon Press, 1961], 79).

67. These are Daix 681, 683 (Fig. 55), 685 (Fig. 63), 686, 689 (Fig. 62), 793. A seventh work using this paper was produced in Avignon (Daix 799).

68. See Christine Poggi's discussion of "Collage and Decoration" in *In Defiance of Painting*, 137–41.

69. Kahnweiler, *Rise of Cubism*, 7.

70. Clement Greenberg, "Avant-Garde and Kitsch," *Art and Culture*, 19–21.

71. Crow writes: "To accept modernism's oppositional claims, we need not assume that it somehow transcends the culture of the commodity; we can see it rather as exploiting to critical purpose contradictions within and between distinct sectors of that culture. . . . The privileged moment of modernist negation occurs . . . when the two aesthetic orders, the high and the low, are forced into scandalous identity. Each of the two positions occupied by the avant-garde artist, the high-cultural and the subcultural, is thereby continuously dislocated by the other. . . . Cubist collage stands as another step in the same direction, its critical character derived from a re-positioning of even more exotically low-brow goods and protocols within the preserve of high art" ("Modernism and Mass Culture," 244–45).

72. In "Cubist Collage and the Culture of Commodities," Christine Poggi places collage within these two parameters of the "decorative" but argues that Picasso was exploiting one of them to challenge the other: employing commodity and kitsch cultural elements in his collages in order to critique the symbolist use of the decorative to achieve the aims of aesthetic purity. Although she points to the internal contradictions possible within the continuation of symbolist aims in Matisse's use of the decorative, she argues that Picasso's collage production maintains its ironic and distanced relation to both the decorative wing of the avant-garde *and* kitsch taste (*In Defiance of Painting*, 137–41).

73. "Matisse's Radio Interview: First Broadcast, 1942," cited in Poggi, *In Defiance of Painting*, 140.

74. Françoise Gilot records Picasso speaking about how deeply the modern style (a term, in English, the French use for *art nouveau*) had penetrated the avant-garde: "We were all Modern-Style artists. There were so many wild, delirious curves in those subway entrances and in all the other Modern-Style manifestations, that I, even though I limited myself almost exclusively to straight lines, was participating in my fashion in the Modern-Style movement" (*Life with Picasso*, 75–76).

75. John Richardson agrees that this is a mantelpiece and that the work in question is a portrait. He says that the sitter is Eva Gouel but gives no documentation for this assumption other than that Eva, hardly a "young girl," was Picasso's companion in Avignon. As for the issue of color, Richardson sees Matisse's *Red Studio* (1911) as the source for what Picasso accomplishes in this work, as well as in the *Green Still Life* (1914): "Color, which had formerly proved so difficult to integrate into cubism, has finally turned out to be the solution rather than the problem. Instead of painting space as if it were palpable, and dissolving forms in it, Picasso could now make do with an expanse of saturated color—an expanse that is flat yet appears to have depth and substance—in which, as *Red Studio* demonstrates, all manner of things could be suspended or to some extent dissolved in the paint's illusory depths" (*A Life of Picasso*, vol. 2, 334–36). Needless to say, the discussion in this chapter of color as a semiological problem for Picasso that pointillism solves in its own special way rules out Richardson's notion of a Matissean, phenomenological "solution."

76. Yve-Alain Bois first called my attention to this surprising analogy between the outpouring of studies preparatory to the *Demoiselles* and that of the *Balconies*, on the occasion of his essay in response to the Musée Picasso's *Demoiselles* exhibition, "Painting as Trauma," *Art in America*, 76 (June 1988), 130–41.

77. Brigitte Léal, "Picasso's Stylistic 'Don Juanism': Still Life in the Dialectic between Cubism and Classicism," in Boggs, *Picasso and Things*, 35.

78. Daix, *Picasso: Life and Art*, 171.

79. Gary Tinterow also insists on the integration in the *Balconies* of cubism and naturalism as "an inevitable consequence of the pictorial implications of cubism," an argument that would seem wholly untenable (see *Collection Berggruen* [Geneva: Fondation GenevArt, 1988], 204).

80. This is argued throughout Leo Steinberg's work on Picasso; see, especially, "The Algerian Women and Picasso at Large," *Other Criteria* (New York: Oxford University Press, 1972). I also argue it in *Passages in Modern Sculpture* (New York: Viking, 1977), ch. 2.

81. Naum Gabo, "Diagram Showing Volumetric (I) and Stereometric (II) Cubes," reproduced in the magazine *Circle* (London), 1937. Constructivism has been placed in quotation marks here to separate out the practice of Gabo and Pevsner from that of the Russian constructivists, such as Rodchenko, who saw the former's work as unrelated to their own aims.

82. Félicien Fagus in the *Revue Blanche* (July 15, 1901), cited by John Richardson, *A Life of Picasso*, vol. 1 (New York: Random House, 1991), 199.

83. Salmon, *Souvenirs sans fin*, vol. 1, 186.

84. Brassaï, *Picasso and Company*, 132 (translation modified).

85. The phrase is Fredric Jameson's, in his discussion of Claude Simon's relation to style in terms of auto-pastiche: *Postmodernism, or The Cultural Logic of Late Capitalism* (Durham: Duke University Press, 1991), 133.

86. Gérard Genette, *Palimpsestes*, 114–5.

87. See Zervos VII, nos. 54–56, 58. For a discussion of these coded references to the onset of his relation to Marie-Thérèse Walter, as he inscribes her initials (M-T) onto the "cubist" still life, the *M* serving as the profile of the guitar, see Lydia Gassman, "Mystery, Magic, and Love in Picasso, 1925–1938: Picasso and the Surrealist Poets" (Ph.D. diss., Columbia University, 1981).

88. The identification of the autobiographical references in *The Three Musicians* to himself, Max Jacob, and Apollinaire was first analyzed by Theodore Reff, "Picasso's *Three Musicians*," *Art in America*, December 1980. For a discussion of the presence of Gris in *The Milliner's Workshop*, see 227 below.

89. This is true of the work throughout 1920 and 1921. It does not occur in 1922 and only occasionally between 1923 and 1927. In 1928, it becomes the norm.

90. Daix, *Picasso: Life and Art*, 203.

91. When Picasso was falling in love with Françoise Gilot he repeatedly urged her to live with him in secret: "You could work up there in tranquillity, and I'd have a secret in my life that no one could take away from me" (Gilot, *Life with Picasso*, 47, 81).

92. Daix, *Picasso: Life and Art*, 225.
93. Wilhelm Boeck and Jaime Sabartès, *Picasso* (New York: Abrams, n.d.), 38.
94. Brassaï, *Picasso and Company*, 100.

DIME NOVELS

1. In his contribution to the catalog for the recent exhibition of Picasso's portraits, Kirk Varnedoe refers to "what has become a canonic interpretive linkage between Picasso's art and his life" ("Picasso's Self-Portraits," in *Picasso and Portraiture: Representation and Transformation*, ed. William Rubin [New York: Museum of Modern Art, 1996], 147).

2. Norman Mailer, *Portrait of Picasso as a Young Man* (New York: Atlantic Monthly Press, 1995). Hereafter citations appear in the text.

3. The friend in question was Carles Casajemas, with whom Picasso was close for several years, sharing a loft-studio in Barcelona. The two of them went to Paris for three months in 1900, but Picasso hustled Casajemas back to Barcelona when he seemed to be having a nervous breakdown as a result of an unconsummated affair with the married Germaine Pichot. Taking Casajemas with him to Malaga, where he could get financial help from his uncle, Picasso began to find his friend's erratic and obsessional behavior unmanageable. Thereupon he arranged passage for Casajemas back to Paris, where the inevitable took place. Rejected by Germaine, Casajemas put a bullet through his head in the belief that he had murdered her.

4. When the *Mona Lisa* was stolen on August 22, 1911, the French newspapers ran appeals for its return with offers of reward; several articles soon also appeared in *Paris Journal*, telling about the return to the newspaper's office, on two separate occasions, of Iberian statues that had also been taken from the Louvre. Connecting these thefts, the police demanded to know the source of the Iberian story, which led them to Géry Pieret and to Apollinaire, for whom the young man had worked as a secretary in 1907. In that period, Pieret had shown two statues he had absconded with from the Louvre to Picasso, who had bought them. Coming back to Paris in August 1911 he appeared on Apollinaire's doorstep and tried to sell another statue to the poet. Apollinaire refused and Pieret then took himself to the offices of *Paris Journal*, returning the statue to them and selling them a story—printed on August 29—of how easy it was to pilfer from the Louvre. Apollinaire

became extremely apprehensive because of the theft of the *Mona Lisa*, Pieret's connection to the newspaper, and the dragnet being set up by the police. So he and Picasso decided to turn Picasso's statues in to the *Paris Journal* offices as well, and the article detailing this ran in early September. It was through their interrogation of the newspaper reporter, whom Francis Steegmuller identifies as none other than André Salmon, that the police were led to Apollinaire, who, arrested on September 9, explained the circumstances of his knowing Pieret and having had, if only briefly, possession of the Iberian sculptures. Picasso, called in to verify Apollinaire's story, was undoubtedly consumed by guilt and afraid of the extent to which Apollinaire might have implicated him. Since neither Picasso nor Apollinaire was a French citizen, they could have been deported for criminal activity. Although Apollinaire, held for five days in prison, didn't say in his immediately published account, "Mes Prisons," that Picasso denied knowing him, that was the rumor that circulated at the time, and much later Picasso himself admitted it. See the article from *Paris-Presse* (June 20, 1959) in which Picasso says of this occasion: "I answered: 'I have never seen this man' " (reprinted in Steegmuller, *Apollinaire: Poet among the Painters*, 218–19).

5. John Berger, *Success and Failure of Picasso* (Middlesex, England: Penguin, 1965). Hereafter citations appear in the text.

6. In his essay on Picasso, collected in the 1913 *Aesthetic Meditations*, Apollinaire writes: "The object, either real or in *trompe-l'oeil*, will doubtless be called upon to play an increasingly important role. It constitutes the internal frame of the painting, marking the limits of its depth just as the frame marks is exterior limits" (*Apollinaire on Art*, 279). For a discussion of Apollinaire's concept of the "inner frame" in relation to Picasso's collage, see Poggi, *In Defiance of Painting*, 61ff.

7. Daix, *Picasso: Life and Work*, 112.

8. *Souvenirs intimes* is introduced and edited by Gilbert Krill, who presents himself as Fernande's godson and recounts that it was Madame Braque who reported the existence of the manuscript, written in the 1950s, to Picasso, who promptly paid Fernande about $20,000 not to publish it. Picasso had earlier tried unsuccessfully to prevent the publication of *Picasso et ses amis* in 1933. Upon Fernande's death in 1966, Krill claims, he found the manuscript in a trunk. Why it was not published until 1988, long after the death of Picasso, Krill doesn't explain. Hereafter citations to *Souvenirs intimes* appear in the text.

9. Olivier, *Picasso and His Friends*, 15.

10. From the account of her adolescence in *Souvenirs intimes*, it is clear that Fernande never visited museums with her family. It is also clear that she had no sympathy whatever for cubism. For example, she tells us of a portrait Picasso made of her in 1907 (in the *Demoiselles d'Avignon* period): "This wholly classical portrait showed his mastery in a genre so opposite to his new experiments. This study, which he would never show to anyone, which he carefully hid in the closet with secret works, calm, sensitive, and severe, I also loved. What has become of it? I now wonder whether he wasn't simply a repressed person who didn't want, couldn't accept this form of art that he denied but which he deeply felt" (222). In *Picasso and His Friends*, this lack of sympathy also emerges: "I have always preferred the work of Derain to that of all the others. His sound and vigorous craftsmanship was unequalled. . . . Derain, though, was a different kind of painter [from Picasso]: more French, more self-confident" (106). Similarly her accounts of literary gatherings are a kind of gush without any sense of what really transpired. Typical is a description of an evening at the Closerie des Lilas: "What life, what uproar, what madness! what interminable discussion, only brought to a halt when the host threw us out into the street" (44).

11. See Alain Corbin, *Le temps, le désir, et l'horreur: Essais sur le dix-neuvième siècle* (Paris: Aubier, 1991), 110; trans. Jean Birrell as *Time, Desire, and Horror: Towards a History of the Senses* (Cambridge, Mass.: Polity Press, 1995).

12. Fernande tells of walking in on her sculptor-lover lying next to a very young nude model, who abruptly gets dressed and leaves, demanding double payment for the sitting. Fernande's reaction is outrage at the price the child is exacting, without admitting to herself—although it is obvious to the reader—that the surcharge is for the sex that her own entrance curtailed (see *Souvenirs*, 122).

13. In Céleste Mogador's *Mémoires de Mogador* (1854), her spectacular rise from *soumise* prostitute (registered with the Paris police) to performer in a dance hall (where she is rebaptized Mogador) to courtesan mistress of the Count Lionel de Chabillan, who finally marries her, is facilitated by her entry into the bohemian world of painters, musicians, and poets who populate "la nouvelle Athène" and who form a milieu in which all classes are allowed to mingle. This social lability understood as uniquely open to artists is dramatized by the character Etienne

Castel of Xavier de Montepin's *La porteuse de pain* (1884), a provincial artist who paints the heroine's picture in the context of their native village and who, twenty years later, himself now a highly cultivated and successful Parisian painter, recognizes her despite the terrifying trials she has had to endure. Indeed, the story and moral turn on this theme of the portrait through which the soul is made available in the face in a manner that only the initiated are able to read: "L'âme se lit sur le visage mais seul les âmes d'élite ont accès à cette connaissance infaillible et intuitive." In one of the subplots Castel becomes involved with an unprincipled fashion model but ends by converting her. See Anne-Marie Thiesse, *Le roman du quotidien: Lecteurs et lectures populaires à la Belle Epoque* (Paris: Le Chemin Vert, 1984), 160–62.

14. Not only is there no mention of the *Demoiselles d'Avignon* anywhere in either of her books, despite the fact that Picasso was doing battle with this canvas for over half a year during the time Fernande was living with him (they separated briefly in the summer and early fall of 1907), but her account of Kahnweiler's first visit to Picasso's studio manages to leave out the dealer's incitement to see Picasso in the first place, namely, the news that was spreading about this important painting.

15. Roman Jakobson, "On a Generation That Squandered Its Poets" (1931), *Verbal Arts, Verbal Sign, Verbal Time* (Minneapolis: University of Minnesota Press, 1985), 124.

16. Ladislav Matejka and Krystyna Pomorska, eds., *Readings in Russian Poetics* (Cambridge: MIT Press, 1971), 52.

17. Mary Matthews Gedo, *Picasso: Art as Autobiography* (Chicago: University of Chicago Press, 1980), 253.

18. William Rubin, *Picasso and Portraiture*, 46.

19. Pierre Cabanne, *Pablo Picasso, His Life and Times*, 252. The reason for assuming that Picasso intended this as a reference to *The Milliner's Workshop*—beyond the painting's being the only candidate to fit the description—focuses on the presence of the male figure entering the door on the right. Despite the current assumptions that this *must* be Picasso (see Rubin, *Picasso and Portraiture*, 62), the figure can be associated with death, since it resembles the black silhouette in *The Dance* of seven months earlier, which Picasso identified as the just-deceased Ramon Pichot (see Roland Penrose, *Picasso, His Life and Work* [New York: Harper and Row, 1973], 258).

20. Picasso told Gilot that Marie-Thérèse was seventeen when they

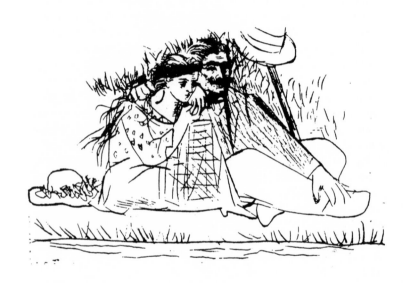

76.
Couple in the Grass
November 17, 1925

met (Gilot, *Life with Picasso*, 235). Marie-Thérèse's account comes from two interviews: Barry Ferrell, "His Women: The Wonder Is That He Found Time to Paint," *Life*, December 27, 1968, 74, and Pierre Cabanne, "Picasso et les joies de la paternité," *L'Oeil*, no. 226 (May 1974), 2–11.

21. See my earlier development of this theory in "Life with Picasso," in *Je suis le cahier: The Sketchbooks of Picasso*, ed. Arnold Glimcher and Marc Glimcher (New York: Pace Gallery, 1986), 113–39.

22. Herbert T. Schwarz, *Picasso and Marie-Thérèse Walter, 1925–1927* (Paris: Editions Isabeau, 1988).

23. The catalog for the 1955 Picasso retrospective at the Musée des Arts Décoratifs, Paris, curated by Maurice Jardot, who had privileged access to Picasso, noted of *The Milliner's Workshop*: "This workshop was in fact located across the street, facing the windows of the apartment where Picasso lived on the rue de la Boétie." Since for this occasion Jardot was changing the title in Zervos, which read only *The Milliners*, it would seem that he did so in conference with the artist. Herbert Schwarz, writing that he has been unable to locate such a workshop, argues that this scene is really set in the living room of Marie-Thérèse's house in the suburb of Maisons Alfort but that Picasso, interested in hiding the fact, was not above giving misinformation (*Picasso and Marie-Thérèse Walter*, 123). Rubin follows him in this conviction, saying, "Picasso certainly resented questions about his private life, especially as regards Marie-Thérèse, for obvious reasons" (*Picasso and Portraiture*, 106).

24. Schwarz, *Picasso and Marie-Thérèse Walter*, 80. Schwarz says that on its reverse the picture has in Picasso's hand, "Started in 1924, finished in February 1925" (132), but if this were the case, it would be hard to understand why Zervos unequivocally places this work in 1924 [Zervos V, no. 357].

The classical nude with short-cropped hair that will later emerge as the Marie-Thérèse type is rehearsed by Picasso as early as 1920 (see Fig. 73).

25. Schwarz, *Picasso and Marie-Thérèse Walter*, 120, 133.

26. Typical of the contrary logics of the "autobiographical" account and of the structuralist one is the example of *Le couple dans l'herbe*, an etching dated November 17, 1925 (Fig. 76). Always assuming that the various visual narratives of this year are based on the presence of the real-life Marie-Thérèse, Schwarz reads this image as auto-depiction

despite the fact, which he admits, that the male personage in the image resembles Manet, author of *Le déjeuner sur l'herbe*, another famous couple-in-the-grass picture (97). He can't imagine that Picasso could be projecting a fantasy in which a major hero of modernism meets the most important model of his life by accident on a busy Paris street, a fantasy based on Manet's encounter with Victorine Meurent, which could later be acted out according to a desire that has already been formed.

27. Cited in Jakobson, *Verbal Arts*, 125.

28. Ibid.

29. Ibid., 115.

30. Ibid., 124–25.

31. Gilot, *Life with Picasso*, 23.

32. This argument about the disjunction between vertical and horizontal as producing a crucial oppositional (or "paradigmatic") pair within Picasso's work is made in "The Motivation of the Sign," 266–72; see also Yve-Alain Bois's discussion of the phenomenon with relation to *Still Life with Chair Caning*, in Bois and Krauss, *Formless: A User's Guide* (New York: Zone Books, 1997), 27–28.

INDEX